Ruth Esau knows leadership. Even "the real essence of leadership." Thi— leadership principles or manual on leadership skills. It is a saturation in the life of Jesus as portrayed in the gospel of Mark, and from that saturation a distillation of Jesus's way as a leader. Many books are written to sharpen us as leaders; this one's written to deepen us.

—*Mark and Cheryl Buchanan*

In *Shifting Perspectives*, Ruth invites the reader on a journey to discover the leadership style of Jesus—and learn to apply His values and approaches when walking with people in their own roles as spiritual guides.

Rather than do all the thinking for us, Ruth uses insightful questions to help us process and then personally hear the call of Jesus's heart—to love, live for, and lay down our lives for those we lead.

We heartily endorse this book and are confident it will become one of your go-to leadership development resources!

—*Ian and Val Byrd,*
leaders of Forerunner Church, Calgary, Alberta,
apostolic team leader of the LifeLinks International Fellowship
of churches and ministries

I have the privilege of calling Ruth a friend, mentor, and former boss. In *Shifting Perspectives*, Ruth describes her mentor Evelyn as someone who "saw where I started from and believed in where I could go." That is exactly how Ruth has impacted my life over the years.

When I first started working for Ruth, I was convinced I was not a leader. However, through gentle pushing and encouragement, I have gone on to lead volunteers, staff teams, and even entire departments. This is largely due to the skills of leadership Ruth demonstrated and drew out of me. I am forever grateful to have her influence in my life.

Shifting Perspectives is not a "free-reading" book. It truly is a resource that you will benefit from—but only if you put in some effort. If you simply read it through, you will miss out. But when you choose to work through the questions, your life will be impacted.

The questions are tough. They are questions I would rather ask others to answer than have to answer myself. But that's the fun of it—being challenged to learn and grow and change. As I have journaled through them, I have identified areas of my leadership that are effective and, other areas that have much room for improvement. Reflecting on these areas and developing a plan for change through the principles outlined in this book has been truly life-changing… and I would highly recommend it.

Ruth, your book challenges me to ponder my influence on others—but then that's the purpose of your endeavour and the book of Mark is a beautiful companion.

This is a thoroughly reflective study intended to grab the heart and mind of shepherds and guide them through self-reflection, bearing the rod of honesty and the staff of transparency. You can quote me on that!

As always, your thoughtfulness makes me dig deep!

—*Deborah Carnduff,*
colleague and friend,
Centre Street Church

Sitting under Ruth's leadership teaching in her Leadership Savvy Cohort (2012–2017), I was encouraged, affirmed, challenged, and spurred on in my ministry leadership positions. In her latest book, *Shifting Perspectives*, based on the leadership style of Jesus Christ, Ruth uses reflections and questions to prompt rich, thought-provoking self-analysis and hope-filled personal steps you can take to embrace new actions and direction in your life.

—*Sandra Tjart,*
former director of EMCC World Partners,
encourager and collaborator for disciples in leadership

As a management student pursuing organizational leadership studies and a practitioner of a coaching-style leadership, I place heightened emphasis on self-awareness and constant improvement. This is mainly because self-awareness enables a person to honestly acknowledge their strengths and weaknesses, and prompts them to seek out ways to constantly improvise.

Ruth's new book, *Shifting Perspectives*, is a refreshing and thought-provoking read which encompasses both of these elements.

Even though I'm not a Christian, I found the elements discussed in the book to be quite motivating from a leadership standpoint. Leaders use a multitude of approaches to inspire followers to deliver the best performance across the board. This book unequivocally prompts readers to hone their self-awareness and self-improvement skills, which is necessary to become better leaders. I highly recommend Ruth's *Shifting Perspectives* without reservation.

—*Sai Raghav, MS, MBA*
Doctoral Learner (Organizational Leadership)
College of Doctoral Studies | University of Phoenix
Inducted Member, Delta Mu Delta (ΔMΔ) International Honour Society for Business and Golden Key International Society
Recipient of the 2019 Lambda Sigma (ΛΣ) Scholarship Award

If leadership is measured in influence, then Jesus of Nazareth is hands down the greatest leader who ever lived. Ruth Esau expertly mines the life and leadership of this Jesus and invites us to consider our own life and leadership in light of His. Written almost devotionally, and in bite-sized but significant portions, this book could (and should) be an important resource for you and the team you lead. This is not a how-to-do leadership book; it's an uplifting how-to-be leadership resource that, when used carefully and thoughtfully, will help transform you, your leadership, and your team from the inside out.

—*Dan and Kerry Wiens*
World Partners, Founders of Inundo

Shifting Perspectives is for all those who want to explore Jesus's leadership practices through His own words and actions. As Christian leaders for many years, we have often been asked the question—and indeed asked the question ourselves: how do I lead like Jesus? This book helps answer that question. It is needed today in our calling to provide leadership in the chaos of the twenty-first century.

Surprisingly, the answer comes from the example of a first-century life recorded by a first-century author. Not surprisingly, it comes from the study, meditation, and life experiences of a woman who has dedicated her life to serving Jesus and helping others serve Him as well. Ruth Esau presents a very personal look into the life of a leader honed through her own experience as a leader, her work with hundreds of leaders over the decades, and her lifelong walk with Jesus. This book reflects Ruth's own discipleship DNA, befriending, loving, conversing, and leading in the way of Jesus.

Shifting Perspectives is a comprehensive look at the leadership principles of Jesus written by a woman who is herself a reflection of the inspired leadership principles communicated in this book. Ruth helps us look with new lenses at the book of Mark to see the leadership principles that will serve us all well. Each section addresses a valuable leadership principle or value, with helpful and insightful questions at the end of each section to help us apply it to our own lives and leadership journeys.

As Christian leaders ourselves, albeit in different environments, the leadership lessons here are universal and are valuable for all Christian leaders on the spectrum of leadership responsibilities. We encourage you to explore *Shifting Perspectives* to grow as you become more like the leader Jesus intended you to be.

—*Heather and Stephen Wile*
Senior Environments Leader, First Alliance Church
Chief Executive Officer, The Mustard Seed

This is not your typical leadership book about how to lead like Jesus. There have been some great ones written, but Ruth Esau brings a unique perspective to the conversation.

In fact, that's what Ruth leads us into—a conversation. She unpacks the gospel of Mark with fresh insights, translating Jesus's way of leading into our current context with practical applications. But she goes beyond that to gift us with perhaps what we need most—the *questions* that will enable us to listen to Jesus's voice speaking into us and shaping us in His way of life and leadership.

Reading and reflecting on this book is like sitting down for a personal coaching session with Ruth. If you sit with the reflections and questions, they will stir you up and reveal what's really going on in your mind and life as a leader, and they will lead you into more of who God has created you to be.

I have known Ruth Esau for almost twenty years and had the privilege of being a pastor under her leadership for a number of those years. She is the real deal as a person, a Jesus follower, and a leader. I have watched as she has identified, raised up, and developed many leaders over the years to become some of the highest quality leaders who have kept leading for the long haul.

She was one of the key leaders who helped me discover and become the person and leader I am today, and she modelled the way for me to raise up and empower other leaders in Jesus's way as well. At times people have said to me, "You ask really good questions that really help me grow!" When they do, I am grateful that at least some of Ruth's way of leadership has stuck with me.

—*Greg Grunau*

Take some down-to-earth common sense, add some homegrown humour, then mix it all with a wonderfully thought-out relational reality touched by love and grace, and you have Ruth Esau wonderful book, *Shifting Perspectives*. In a day when there seems to be an overabundance of leadership books, Ruth encourages us to look at the people and situations around us in a fresh and new way. Suddenly, this is less about leadership and more about building Christ-centred relationships with the added benefit of accomplishing great things together. Highly recommended. This should be high on your list of good books to read this year!

—*Rev. Dr. Kenneth W. DeMaere*

The anchor of faith resident in Ruth's life resonates in the fabric of *Shifting Perspectives*. Ruth writes as she lives, demonstrating a fearless interrogation of her own leadership journey. She provides lessons that guide the reader in creating space to consider what it means to lead in this dizzying time. Ruth's words are gracefully persuasive, compelling the reader to balance each principle through the leadership lens of Jesus. It is a sabbath for the leadership soul. In Ruth's words, this book "gives space to develop a heart that is optimistically realistic." That's exactly the kind of leader our world needs today.

—*Scott Lanigan,*
Executive Pastor, Trinity Church, Kelowna, British Columbia

SHIFTING PERSPECTIVES

Jesus Through A Leadership Lens

Ruth Esau

The Kaleidoscope Leadership Series

SHIFTING PERSPECTIVES
Copyright © 2022 by Ruth Esau

All rights reserved. Neither this publication nor any part of this publication may be reproduced or transmitted in any form or by any means, electronic or mechanical, including photocopying, recording or any information storage and retrieval system, without permission in writing from the author.

Scripture quotations are taken from the Holy Bible, New Living Translation, copyright ©1996, 2004, 2015 by Tyndale House Foundation. Used by permission of Tyndale House Publishers, Carol Stream, Illinois 60188. All rights reserved. Scripture quotations marked MSG are taken from THE MESSAGE, copyright © 1993, 2002, 2018 by Eugene H. Peterson. Used by permission of NavPress, represented by Tyndale House Publishers. All rights reserved.

Printed in Canada

Soft cover ISBN: 978-1-4866-2123-1
Hardcover ISBN: 978-1-4866-2251-1
eBook ISBN: 978-1-4866-2124-8

Word Alive Press
119 De Baets Street Winnipeg, MB R2J 3R9
www.wordalivepress.ca

WORD ALIVE
—P R E S S—

MIX
Paper from
responsible sources
FSC
www.fsc.org   FSC® C103567

Cataloguing in Publication information can be obtained from Library and Archives Canada.

*Dedicated with love and deep gratitude to Evelyn Street,
professor, mentor, and dear friend,
who saw in me what I could not see myself.*

ACKNOWLEDGMENTS	xiii
PREFACE	xv
HOW TO BENEFIT MOST FROM THIS BOOK	xxi
INTRODUCTION: WHY JESUS?	xxv
THE WAY PREPARED	xxxi
APPROVED BY GOD THE FATHER	xxxv

PART ONE: FACING YOUR CRITICS — 1

CHAPTER ONE: THE WISDOM TO KNOW HOW, WHY, AND WHEN TO DEAL WITH YOUR CRITICS	4
CHAPTER TWO: MISSING THE HEART OF THE MATTER	7
CHAPTER THREE: LIVING BY YOUR VALUES WHEN CRITICIZED	10
CHAPTER FOUR: FALSELY ACCUSED	13
CHAPTER FIVE: LET SILENCE DO THE HEAVY LIFTING	16

PART TWO: PRINCIPLES OF GROWTH — 19

CHAPTER SIX: HOW GROWTH ORIENTED ARE YOU?	21
CHAPTER SEVEN: THE ROLE OF THE FARMER AS TEACHER	25
CHAPTER EIGHT: GROWTH IS THE MINDSET OF A KINGDOM BUILDER	29
CHAPTER NINE: STORMS REVEAL OUR GROWTH MORE THAN OUR LEARNING	32

PART THREE: LIVING BY YOUR PRIORITIES — 35

CHAPTER TEN: PERSPECTIVE IN SOLITUDE	38
CHAPTER ELEVEN: WHAT VIEWPOINT DO YOU SEE?	42
CHAPTER TWELVE: THE RHYTHMS OF PUBLIC AND PRIVATE LIFE	45
CHAPTER THIRTEEN: FREEDOM TO CHOOSE	48
CHAPTER FOURTEEN: DEVASTATION IS THE TIME TO SPEAK HOPE	51

PART FOUR: RISK MANAGEMENT — 55

CHAPTER FIFTEEN: DINNER WITH SCUM	57
CHAPTER SIXTEEN: UNDERSTANDING WINESKINS	61
CHAPTER SEVENTEEN: PREPARED TO BALANCE MINISTRY AND POWER	64
CHAPTER EIGHTEEN: WHAT DO PIGS HAVE TO DO WITH RISK MANAGEMENT?	67

PART FIVE: RELATIONAL WEALTH — 71

- CHAPTER NINETEEN: WHO IS MY FAMILY? — 74
- CHAPTER TWENTY: KNOW WHEN TO WALK AWAY — 77
- CHAPTER TWENTY-ONE: PERCEPTION VERSUS REALITY — 79
- CHAPTER TWENTY-TWO: CHILDLIKE, NOT CHILDISH — 82
- CHAPTER TWENTY-THREE: A BEAUTIFUL PATTERN FOR FAREWELL — 85
- CHAPTER TWENTY-FOUR: THE POWER TO SPEAK TRUTH — 89
- CHAPTER TWENTY-FIVE: WHEN CLOSE RELATIONSHIPS DISAPPOINT — 92
- CHAPTER TWENTY-SIX: THE ULTIMATE PRICE OF LEADERSHIP — 95

PART SIX: UNDERSTANDING POWER AND AUTHORITY — 99

- CHAPTER TWENTY-SEVEN: TEACHING WITH AUTHORITY — 101
- CHAPTER TWENTY-EIGHT: BRAVE DEPENDENCE ON GOD LACED WITH HUMBLE AUTHORITY — 103
- CHAPTER TWENTY-NINE: UNBELIEF KILLS POWER — 106
- CHAPTER THIRTY: HEAVENLY POWER — 109
- CHAPTER THIRTY-ONE: THE TENSION BETWEEN THE POWER OF JESUS' NAME AND THE POWER OF SIN — 112
- CHAPTER THIRTY-TWO: KEEP WATCH AND PRAY — 115

PART SEVEN: EMPOWERING OTHERS — 119

- CHAPTER THIRTY-THREE: AS HE WAS WALKING — 121
- CHAPTER THIRTY-FOUR: CHOOSING YOUR LEADERS — 124
- CHAPTER THIRTY-FIVE: HOW DO YOU LISTEN — 127
- CHAPTER THIRTY-SIX: INSTRUCTIONS FOR THE JOURNEY — 130
- CHAPTER THIRTY-SEVEN: CHOOSE TO EMPOWER YOUR FOLLOWERS — 133
- CHAPTER THIRTY-EIGHT: CHALLENGING SCARCITY MINDSETS — 136
- CHAPTER THIRTY-NINE: RELATIONAL PING PONG — 139

PART EIGHT: POWERFUL STORYTELLING — 141

- CHAPTER FORTY: STORYTELLING — 143
- CHAPTER FORTY-ONE: MEANINGFUL ILLUSTRATIONS — 146
- CHAPTER FORTY-TWO: EMBEDDING THE LEARNING — 149

CHAPTER FORTY-THREE: INVITE CONFLICT AS A TOOL FOR LEARNING	152
CHAPTER FORTY-FOUR: TEACHABLE MOMENTS	155

PART NINE: EMOTIONAL INTELLIGENCE — 157

CHAPTER FORTY-FIVE: HARD HEARTS ARE CHALLENGED	158
CHAPTER FORTY-SIX: HEATED EMOTIONS	161
CHAPTER FORTY-SEVEN: HANGRY JESUS	165
CHAPTER FORTY-EIGHT: HANDLING STRESSFUL EMOTIONS	167
CHAPTER FORTY-NINE: EMOTIONS AND FACTS WORK TOGETHER	170

PART TEN: OUR FRIEND, SAVIOUR, AND LEADER — 175

CHAPTER FIFTY: EGO BLINDS TRUE PERSPECTIVE AND LEAVES US EMPTY	176
CHAPTER FIFTY-ONE: WHO GETS THE GLORY	180
CHAPTER FIFTY-TWO: WHEN LEADERSHIP LEADS TO DEATH, METAPHORICALLY OR IN REALITY	182
CHAPTER FIFTY-THREE: OUR SAVIOUR, LORD, LEADER, AND GUIDE	190
CONCLUSION	193
RESOURCES	197
FROM THE AUTHOR	199

ACKNOWLEDGMENTS

AS I SAT to write this book, I was reminded of the privilege and responsibility I had to invest in, empower, and entrust ministry to the women who came into my area of influence in Women's Ministry at Centre Street Church from 1996 to 2007. I acknowledge that as I worked with this wonderful team of women over the years, they spurred me on to be an ever-growing leader who poured into them so they could pour out upon and through others. As a result of their faithfulness to their call and role in women's ministry, I now have the privilege of having spiritual grandchildren to at least the fourth generation.

Thank you, CSC Women's Leadership Team Members from 1996 to 2007, for your faithful service.

Thank you to Vidette Heller, Kelly Krieger, Mary Lee Pedora, Barb Kempers, Beth Mclean Wiest, Marlene Fritzler, Sally Walls, Carol Grant, Glenda Lenz, Kerry Wiens, Deb Carnduff, Rosemary Flaaten, Dianne, Dorothy Cowling, Joyce Anquist, Phyllis Teske, Tannis Melville-Oberten, Jacqueline Nadworny, Verdeen Bueckert, Cheyene Archer, Marilyn Shellenberg, Marjorie Tetz, Cindy Martin, Charlotte Riegle, Dee McGinnis, Angie Beers, Pamela Sylvenski, Dixie Crouse, and Gail Kirwin.

I also extend deep thanks and appreciation to my dear partner in life and love, Brian. You have been and so truly are the wind beneath my feet in so many practical and meaningful ways. You are the holder of my heart and encourager all the way.

As I have laboured through and written *Shifting Perspectives*, I have been blessed. I am grateful for and deeply treasure the friendship, mentorship. and wise questioning and editing of Joanne Wiens.

I am grateful for Vidette Heller—her generous spirit, sharp eye, wise suggestions, and knowing heart.

Mark Buchanan, wow! You stretched me out of my comfort zone and breathed new life into my words and way of expressing them. Thank you. Your wealth and depth of wisdom and humour have been an inspiration. I am grateful that our paths crossed in this significant way.

Word Alive Press has provided me with invaluable support and the expertise of such wise people. For one, Evan Braun, developmental editor and copy editor. Thank you, Evan, for getting the heart of where I was going and giving me permission to hone and become a storyteller with purpose. What started as such a sparse manuscript became richer and deeper because of your investment in it and in me as an author. Thank you to the Word Alive Press team of Jen Jandavs-Hedlin, Marina Reis (project manager extraordinaire), and those I never met who worked behind the scenes to bring this manuscript to life. Your time and expertise is greatly appreciated.

I am blessed with prayer warriors on many sides and am most grateful for each one. You are my source of inspiration, energy, momentum, and sweet accountability. Thank you for your friendship and prayers.

I am indebted to the non-profit sector of Calgary, where I am privileged to teach, facilitate, and coach amazing leaders from many organizations who are difference makers in our city and world.

To the many authors, teachers, preachers, speakers, mentors, coaches, and friends I know: you have enriched and deepened my life. As all of these learnings have come together here, please know that I have attempted to acknowledge where my learnings have come from. Please forgive me for any lapses in giving credit where credit is due.

PREFACE

"CURIOSITY KILLED THE cat; satisfaction brought it back." How often I heard these words as a nine- or ten-year-old.

We had recently welcomed a new minister to our church. Although I was well-versed in faith and Bible stories, Reverend McPhee used language and ideas beyond my ability to grasp. I constantly wanted to put my hand up and ask, "What does that mean?"

One Sunday on the way out of church, I approached Reverend McPhee. He was intimidating in his long, black-pleated robe with puffy sleeves and a hard white circular collar that seemed to hold his head high.

In spite of my intimidation, my curiosity was strong. As I reached to shake the hand he held out to me, I timidly asked, "Reverend McPhee, you use a lot of big words that I don't understand. If I wrote them in a notebook, would you write out their meaning for me?"

"Yes."

At Woolworths, I bought a new little flip wire notebook. I could hardly wait for Sunday.

When Sunday finally arrived, I was sitting up straight, my notebook open and my pencil sharpened, waiting for the first big word I didn't understand. Words like covenant, dogma, ecumenical, infallible, inerrant, metanoia, inductive, deductive, and relativism. There were many. So many.

After the service, I was no longer intimidated, just excited to hand my questions to Reverend McPhee. He graciously shook my hand and accepted my little notebook.

On Wednesday evening as my family arrived for the prayer service, he handed me back my notebook. I quickly opened it and saw his handwritten answers.

I don't remember how long we kept up our Q&A. What I do remember is my thirst to know more, and that my minister didn't turn me away, young as I was.

Curiosity killed the cat; satisfaction brought it back.

That persistent thirst to know more, be more, and live more has been an integral part of my leadership journey. Searching out great resources that resonate with my heart and thereby create opportunities for my thoughts to shift and move forward has become an important part of who I am as a leader. I feel a persistent hunger to walk with others as they discover who God created them to be, to learn that He has given them a call and a purpose that serves something so much bigger than themselves.

My persistent encounters with Jesus and the ways of Jesus have transformed my life. They call me to invite, invest in, and entrust to others in a way that frees them to explore and become all they were created and called to be.

There is no shortage of books on leadership as seen through the filter of those who've been there and done that. Many great and inspiring resources are at our fingertips, yet we still hunger for more when it comes to leadership that makes people worthy to follow.

Many great and public leaders have succumbed to what John describes in 1 John 2:16: *"For the world offers only a craving for physical pleasure, a craving for everything we see, and pride in our achievements and possessions."* We have become disillusioned with the process of finding leaders to emulate, and so we to search for more. Many leadership-focused books and authors have stretched me and given me the opportunity to continually broaden, question, and grow.

My curiosity and desire to ask deep questions has led me to consider the life of one of the world's greatest leaders, Jesus Christ. Having come to a personal relationship with Jesus as a young child, and using His teachings as the foundation of my life, I chose to look at the book of Mark and glean leadership lessons from His teaching and the way He lived His life.

Mark, although not one of Jesus's twelve disciples, definitely was a fervent follower of Jesus Christ. In Acts 13:13, we see that Mark accompanied Paul on his very first missionary journey. Mark's portrayal of Jesus is as an adult and as a leader, and through Mark's eyes we see Jesus for who He was and how He lived out the mandate His Father gave Him.

The key passage for those who seek to understand Jesus's leadership style is presented in Mark 10:43–45. Mark was trying to help them see that leadership through Jesus's lens was different.

If you want to lead, you must first serve.

If you think being first counts most, you're going to have to be a slave to everyone else.

Jesus was clear about His purpose. He didn't expect everyone to serve Him, and they didn't. In his life, he set a new pace, a new model of serving others even to the point of giving His life so others—in fact, many—could be ransomed.

Jesus, the Son of the living God who had every right to the position of entitlement, chose to come as a servant of all. Throughout the book of Mark, we are given opportunities to work through rich and varied stories to see Jesus in action and witness how He lived out the true meaning of servant leadership. This is our template for living fruitful and fulfilling leadership lives.

Shifting Perspectives was written to give you bite-sized leadership insights and entice you into a new way of seeing Jesus and understanding how He led. My hope is that you will embrace what resonates with you personally and professionally and allow it to penetrate your thinking and attitudes and transform your leadership style and effectiveness.

As I pondered this leadership study, I became fascinated to see that God's call on Jesus's heart wasn't limited to one ministry, one program, or one church. Jesus's call was to be lived wherever He was. It was the central part of who He was.

The challenge to us when we leave a leadership position may be to question our call, but in fact those are opportunities to reaffirm who God created us to be and seek His heart for how and where we are to live out that call. His clearest call to us is to follow His heart and allow Him to breathe His very life in and through us. That requires us to pay attention to Him, His ways, and His purposes.

That is what we will discover along our journey through Mark.

As we begin Mark's gospel, you may recall that the Passover celebration was near. Excitement and anticipation was at an all-time high. Jesus walked into the world of a few chosen ones and turned their lives upside down, seriously challenging what they knew and expected from religious leaders. Most compelling is that those who came in touch with Jesus knew beyond a shadow of a doubt how deeply they were loved. They were seen for who they were, and they were called by name.

As I pondered the rest of the story, I found it profound and thought-provoking. All I can say is that I experienced a sense of amazement; what appeared to be the end of Jesus's life is revealed to be only the beginning of new life and grace offered to all.

What a picture this is of my Jesus, the one who has created me, called me by name, and given me purpose. I have fallen in love with Him and long for those in my circle of influence to fall in love with Him as well and live their Jesus story to the fullest.

The story we hear in John 13 showcases the brilliant clarity of Mark's challenge to us: to be different, and if we want to be leaders we must also be servants.

I wonder, do you wish you could grasp this man and His leadership style and approach? Do you wonder what gave Him that strong and stable ability to do what He knew was pleasing to His Father even while facing the deepest betrayal of His life? Do you wonder about how He could be so assured in His identity, purpose, and accountability?

Three principles really stand out for me in the book of Mark. They lay the foundation for how I perceive Jesus's leadership.

The first is His relational bent. Jesus's purpose came from the relationship He had with His Father, and it extended to how and why it mattered in His relationships with His disciples and with the people who were in His circle of influence.

Secondly, Jesus's strong focus was on empowering others. He knew what He had been put on this earth to do. He knew and had confidence in the relationship He had with His Father and in the fact that He had been sent and empowered with authority by His Father. This is what He wanted His followers to feel and to grasp.

Thirdly, He had a desire and willingness to be accountable. He recognized that He would be returning to His Father and would be answerable for what He had done during His time here on the earth. He had a deep need for relationship with His Father and was empowered by His Father to live in healthy accountability.

Mark creates this challenge for us to consider. What is so different in Jesus's leadership style and our culture's view of leadership? How do we discover Jesus's leadership style? Why does this understanding matter to our call to fulfill His purpose for us according to His creation of us?

Please come with me and follow in the leadership footsteps of this amazing man, Jesus.

HOW TO BENEFIT MOST FROM THIS BOOK

WHAT IF A slight move or turn created a shift in our thinking that freed us up to see from a new perspective and make space for fresh momentum in our lives?

A cozy blanket, a beloved doll, a fur-trimmed pink parka, a loving home... they all add up to an idealistic picture of life for a toddler.

Now flip the picture: excruciating stomach pain, screaming in agony, harried and worried parents...

At age three, I was stricken with a sudden onset of rheumatic fever. Life changed. Medical appointments and weekly blood tests resulted in a lengthy hospital stay for me. Then I was confined to bedrest for a year. I had to take a pink medicine with a cherry in the bottom to entice me to drink it all. I could no longer run, jump, or play rambunctiously. Instead a favourite hospital pastime was playing with a little metal doll that crawled across my blankets and made me giggle. There were also times of quiet colouring or doing puzzles.

Some sixty-eight years later, I wonder how my parents entertained this curious, spunky three-year-old. In my mind's eye, I see the barred metal crib that was my living space for a year. My parents moved it under the kitchen window to broaden my view during the day—and when it was warm, they moved it to the front lawn where the neighbourhood kids played around me. My mom made a scrapbook to hold all the precious cards and memories of those days.

One gift I received was a kaleidoscope. I loved it, especially on days when my crib was moved outside or close to the kitchen window. I loved the beauty I saw when I looked through the eyepiece. If I moved the kaleidoscope up to the sky, the colours became vibrant and bright. If I pointed it down to the blankets, the colours became much more subdued and gentle. If I got tired of the pattern, the tiniest twist would shift the design and I'd see something I hadn't seen before.

As an adult, I immersed myself in leadership, but I still saw life through kaleidoscopes as I sought to help the people in my influence better understand these principles.

If a small twist of a kaleidoscope could produce something so different, could I not use it as a metaphor to bring understanding to how we navigate those times when we find ourselves stuck in leadership situations that seem impossible?

As I analyzed the make-up of a kaleidoscope, I made some wonderful discoveries. The ever-changing beauty in a kaleidoscope comes from the many broken pieces of glass that comprise it, as well as the light and mirrors that are needed to shift the patterns. Light is such a crucial component of the shifting view.

Leadership has many universal principles—and no matter our role, situation, relationships, or context, these universal principles apply. When we get stuck, we just need a little twist of insight or change of direction to reveal the possibilities that lie ahead.

The kaleidoscope has become a metaphor for so much in my world of leadership development. Many kaleidoscopic discoveries awaited me. For example, I had to accept that I didn't know what I didn't know. Things changed when I allowed my perspective to shift, often resulting in a new perspective to marvel at.

It also became evident that failure is never the end. I found that I could use my mistakes and failures as a leader to launch me to new levels of influence.

In addition, I learned that reflections keep us true to our higher purpose. If I made more time for intentional reflection, weighing what is with what could be, where might it take me?

As you work your way through *Shifting Perspectives*, you'll come face to face with similar questions that are intended to empower you to find that new view, shift your focus, and get you unstuck. You will find these challenging questions under each section's Kaleidoscope Reflections. I invite you not to jump over them, but to use them to create space to grow and become all you were intended to be.

As I invite you to read the book of Mark, your first shift in thinking will be to read it through leadership eyes rather than theological eyes. You'll be amazed when you read passages such as the one in which Jesus watches His disciples struggle in the storm, or when Jesus lives out His last moments before going to the cross.

Changing the lens through which you view these stories will stop you in your tracks. Ask yourself, would any of the leaders you know invest or lead in these ways? Would you invest or lead these ways? Jesus put His all on the line for the call of His Father and the purposes He was sent for and the joy of His return to His Father when His work was complete.

Shifting Perspectives is thematic in its style. It doesn't need to be read from front to back in the order that it was written. Instead:

1. Choose the theme you want to focus on.
2. Read the suggested passage three to five times, and read it through a leadership lens. Focus on what you see of Jesus's thoughts, attitudes, and behaviours as they apply to leadership. Don't skip this step, even if you feel that you know the story. God's Word is alive and ready to meet you each time you step into it.
3. Have a notebook and pen handy to work through the Kaleidoscope Reflections. These are intended to enable you to be more strategic in your thinking and come to conclusions about how each passage and story can inform your leadership context.
4. Create challenging and productive conversations for developing clear, strategic thinking with your people and your teams.

Join me in this challenging and fascinating journey with Jesus, the world's greatest leader. Take the time to reflect and grapple with the truths you discover. Allow them to change and deepen your leadership. Then share what you've gained with others. Entrusting life lessons to others includes allowing them to embrace God's principles to go through the processes that will move them forward and allow God to bear His truth in their heart for His purposes.

Be blessed as you intentionally walk this learning road and entrust to others the benefit of your renewed understanding and shifting perspectives.

INTRODUCTION
WHY JESUS?

THIS BOOK BEGAN as I sat at the senior pastors' table of a large church where I served in the area of life transformation. The initial idea came as I searched for leadership development material to inspire my leaders that was concise, clear, and thought-provoking.

When I couldn't find what I was looking for, I began to better understand the opportunity I had been given to write principle-based leadership development material that could be readily translated into any context of ministry. I didn't want to write in a format that caused the reader to search for the right answers; I wanted a format that would instead give leaders an opportunity to develop their thinking skills and become more strategic and intentional according to God's revealed purposes. I wanted them to internalize His work in their lives.

This is not a work that looks for all the correct answers. It is a work that seeks to create space for you to reflect and shift your thinking, to weigh the picture of Jesus as a leader and take His principles into your context and setting. It will invite you to learn to lead by being firmly established in God's Word and open to His movement and direction in your midst.

We are blessed to have the Old Testament as our firm foundation to build upon, and yet we also live in the age of grace. We experience the privilege and responsibility of having Jesus, through the power and anointing of His precious Holy Spirit as our constant companion on the journey.

We see His Father's heart and purposes in John 5:19, in which we read that Jesus knew He could do nothing by Himself. He knew that He was to lean heavily into what He observed His Father doing. Then He chose to do the same.

Jesus was deliberate in His leadership and in how He taught and drew His disciples into His leadership world. His purpose was clear, His time was short, and there was much to be done.

Jesus knew that for His Father's Kingdom to come (Matthew 6:10), the Kingdom would have to be built in ever-increasing ways, by building relationships with those He led and walked with. The Kingdom grew even further through Jesus's direct teaching and empowering of His followers, entrusting to them His Father's ways and seeing that they walked in the accountability of obedience to God.

So, why use Jesus as the role model for effective and transformative leadership? Perhaps you're beginning to see that Jesus's style, attitudes, and behaviours all speak to the power of knowing where you've come from, who you are, what you are to do, and who you will be returning to after all is said and done. This is an empowered and accountable life.

You are invited to join me as we look more deeply and embrace Jesus and His leadership style through the eyes of Mark.

In Mark 10:43–45, Jesus reminded the disciples that, for them, leadership would be turned on its head. It would be different. It would mean serving others.

His words seemed hard for them to understand. He told them that if they wanted to lead, they needed to learn to be like a slave. He was shaking them out of their indignation by telling them that even He, as the Son of Man, hadn't come to be served but to serve and give His life so others could be ransomed.

John 13:1–20 sets the stage for our leadership journey through Mark. Here we see this story of profound and deeply meaningful leadership unfold through the eyes of a young woman who was called to serve that evening.

I was preparing the room for Jesus and his disciples. He had specifically asked for a large basin of water and a towel, and as the servant girl for this household I put the final touches onto the preparations in the upper room they were to use.

Jesus had been in and out of our city for a number of years. People talked about His amazing teaching and ability to heal people of all kinds of diseases. He even cast out demons!

Whenever I overheard others speak of Him, I felt shivers go up and down my spine, sensing the wonder of the possibility. What if He was who He said He was, the Son of God?

As I observed and listened to the disciples as they gathered around Jesus, I came to realize that He had known all along this was going to be a deeply troubling evening for Him and those He loved. He knew that the time was coming soon for Him to leave His loved ones. He also knew that one of His chosen followers was about to betray Him.

Honestly, I tremble to imagine what it would be like to do what He did, knowing I would be betrayed by someone I trusted and believed in. That truly is the kind of God-sized love that I have yet to grow into. I have a long way to go.

As I listened from the sidelines, I became aware that Jesus also knew He had been sent by His Father to accomplish His Father's will. He had been given authority by His Father over everything. Jesus knew, too, that soon He was going to return to His Father.

Because of what Jesus knew, I leaned in to watch Him get up from the table. He removed His robe, wrapped a towel around His waist, and poured water into a basin. I was intrigued! What on earth was He going to do now? I knew to expect the unexpected, yet that didn't make it any less startling or heart-stopping for me.

"Breathe," I told myself as I gulped for air. "Just breathe."

Slowly, while Jesus walked around the table, He stopped. With a deep look of love, He bent on one knee before John, then paused and looked deeply into John's eyes.

I saw John squirm in his seat. I can only imagine what he was thinking.

Jesus tenderly lifted one of John's dusty feet and one at a time placed each one in the basin, washing away all the dust and grime of the day. Just as gently, He dried John's feet with the towel He had around His waist. It was an intimate and holy moment.

I found myself holding my breath again. As Jesus stood, I exhaled slowly, feeling the warmth of tears trickle down my cheeks. I could hardly see as Jesus got up and one by one washed and dried the feet of each of His other disciples.

Oh, I almost forgot: when Jesus came to wash Simon Peter's feet, there was another momentary breath-holding moment. Peter actually challenged Jesus.

Really, Peter! How could you?

Peter said to Jesus, "Lord, are you going to wash my feet?"

Jesus looked him in the eye. "You don't understand now what I'm doing, but someday you will."

"No. You will never, ever wash my feet!"

Jesus gently held Peter's foot and looked into his eyes. "Peter, if I don't wash your feet, you will not belong to Me."

That caught Simon Peter's attention and he blurted, "Well, Lord, if that's true, then wash my hands and head, not just my feet."

Very patiently, Jesus paused and held Peter's gaze. "Oh Peter, if you only understood. If a person has already bathed, they only need to wash their feet to be clean." There was a moment of heavy silence as Jesus regarded the rest of the disciples and declared, "Not all of you are clean."

This was the piece I was telling you about. It was overwhelming to realize that Jesus knew who would betray Him, and it was a person in that very room. Can you imagine?

This amazing man finished washing their feet, put on his robe again, and sat down.

"Do you understand what I was doing?" Jesus asked.

I'm uncertain how to describe His tone since I was so amazed at what was happening.

Jesus then said to them, "You call me 'Teacher' and 'Lord,' and you're right, because that's what I am."

He was so strong in His identity, with no apologies or excuses.

"And since I, your Lord and Teacher, have washed your feet, you ought to wash each other's feet," He continued. "This is My example that I want you to follow: do as I have done to you."

I got so lost in thinking about this amazing man and His unexplainable attitude and demeanour. All I can say is it was a hushed and holy moment that seemed to linger. I wanted to hold onto the moment until I really understood it, to give some kind of definition to what I had just seen. I wanted to be with this man and have Him see me, to call me by name; I wanted to know that I was invited to be one of His.

As the disciples drifted out of the room and I started to gather things up, my eyes followed them, longing to stay in His presence, to be known by Him the way a true follower would be.

As I wrote this, I imagined that I was that young woman called to serve. Sadly, I wasn't. I know you weren't there either, and so I invite you to journey with me as we observe Jesus through a lens of leadership in the rest of the book of Mark.

THE WAY PREPARED

This is the Good News about Jesus the Messiah, the Son of God. It began just as the prophet Isaiah had written: "Look, I am sending my messenger ahead of you, and he will prepare your way. He is a voice shouting in the wilderness, 'Prepare the way for the Lord's coming! Clear the road for him!'"

This messenger was John the Baptist. He was in the wilderness and preached that people should be baptized to show that they had repented of their sins and turned to God to be forgiven. All of Judea, including all the people of Jerusalem, went out to see and hear John. And when they confessed their sins, he baptized them in the Jordan River. His clothes were woven from coarse camel hair, and he wore a leather belt around his waist. For food he ate locusts and wild honey.

John announced: "Someone is coming soon who is greater than I am—so much greater that I'm not even worthy to stoop down like a slave and untie the straps of his sandals. I baptize you with water, but he will baptize you with the Holy Spirit!"

(Mark 1:1–8)

THE CONCEPT OF preparation is common for most of us, albeit perhaps in different ways. For example, today I prepared:

- the place I love to sit for my quiet times each morning.
- my breakfast.
- for the day with daily habits.
- for the day with journaling and Scripture reading.
- my desk for my teaching session from 9:00–12:00.

It often seems that life is all about planning, preparation, and actually making our plans work. It's a continuum similar to what we face daily as we run our home and use it, often, for hospitality. Without some form of planning and preparation, there would be no snacks in the cupboard, no guests at the table, and no food for guests to eat.

It seems simple, yet do we grasp how much time we spend making these kinds of decisions—and even weightier decisions?

Then there are times when we prepare a place for family or friends to come and be with us. The hospitality of our hearts wants to prepare a place that says, "I have waited for you. I'm so glad you are here. I can't wait to see you."

Mark 1 relates the history and story of John the Baptist and his call to prepare the way for Jesus, the Son of God, and His earthly ministry. John also prepared the people for the expanded ministry of Jesus that was to come with and through the power of the Holy Spirit.

John was very aware that he was to prepare others for Jesus's presence and leadership. This preparation wasn't just for the beginning of Jesus's earthly ministry, but also was for the ministry to continue when Jesus was no longer on the earth.

As leaders, our role is not to simply do the ministry but to prepare others to rise to be all they were created to be. We are to help others grow and develop into who God created them to be and what He called them to do, knowing that when they see Him, their reward will be to hear, "Well done, good and faithful servant."

John prepared the way for Jesus, a leader greater than himself. We have no idea if the people we are called to influence, empower, and walk with will be greater than us or not. That doesn't really matter. What matters is our faithfulness in obeying the Lord as He works in and through us to empower others and walk with them in accountability to God's purposes.

Mark gives us an opportunity to see Jesus through leadership eyes and embrace His influence for ourselves and others.

KALEIDOSCOPE REFLECTIONS

1. In what ways have you benefitted from another leader's preparation for what you are to do?

2. When you think of preparing others for fulfilling their calling, what stands out most to you in this passage?

3. What is it that resonates with your heart? Why does that matter?

4. How has someone prepared the way for you to lead?

5. How are you actually preparing the way for others to lead?

6. What is something Jesus did that your heart longs to embrace and step out in faith to lead with?

APPROVED BY GOD THE FATHER

One day Jesus came from Nazareth in Galilee, and John baptized him in the Jordan River. As Jesus came up out of the water, he saw the heavens splitting apart and the Holy Spirit descending on him like a dove. And a voice from heaven said, "You are my dearly loved Son, and you bring me great joy."

The Spirit then compelled Jesus to go into the wilderness, where he was tempted by Satan for forty days. He was out among the wild animals, and angels took care of him.

Later on, after John was arrested, Jesus went into Galilee, where he preached God's Good News. "The time promised by God has come at last!" he announced. "The Kingdom of God is near! Repent of your sins and believe the Good News!"

(Mark 1:9–15)[1]

LONG BEFORE HE began His earthly ministry, Jesus received the approval of God, His Heavenly Father. This approval was revealed as the Holy Spirit rested on Jesus in the form of a dove.

In this passage, we see that approval is tightly bound together with depth of relationship. Jesus received His Heavenly Father's approval for who He was long before He received approval for what He had done!

What's intriguing to me is that although Jesus held the full approval of God before His ministry began, the Holy Spirit led Him into the wilderness where He faced great temptation and testing.

We tend to fantasize about the life we'll lead as we answer God's call. The prospect of temptation and testing rarely enters our thinking.

---

[1] See also Luke 4:1–11 and Matthew 4:1–11.

We tend to be idealistic, thinking that if God gave us the dream, it will come to pass readily and easily. Dream the dream, see the vision, and there you have it!

And yet dreaming is the easy part. Implementing the dream is the hard work that will take us through temptation and testing to victory and fulfillment!

As I look at my own life story, I see many examples of God's gracious provision, protection, and leadership in my life. I too can see how God prepared the way for me; and because He was my creator, I also knew that I carried a sense of His approval. My greatest gift has been God's faithfulness, presence (whether I felt it or not), and grace even in the midst of the greatest heartbreak and disappointment.

Born and raised in the small town of Trail, British Columbia, I was blessed to be the youngest daughter of Wilma and Russel Johnstone. I came as an added blessing, just two days before my mom's fortieth birthday, a second daughter to complete this family of four.

My parents had met later in life and were clear in their identities, values, and beliefs. The values of integrity, consistency, loyalty, fun, hospitality, family, and a deep love of Jesus marked the decisions they made as a couple and as parents. This was the environment in which I was nurtured and raised.

My faith was grounded through this influence and I felt that I had a real relationship with Jesus. I knew I could call on Him, talking with Him as a friend and faithful provider. I often found myself picturing Jesus and me walking hand in hand, just talking about what came into our hearts and minds.

As a child in elementary school, I once earned an award for scripture memory. The gift was a little copy of Robert Boyd Munger's book, *My Heart, Christ's Home*. Over the years, this little book profoundly captured my heart and imagination, particularly its story of Jesus waiting for us each morning in the living room. It struck me that He waits and longs for me.[2]

---

[2] Robert Boyd Munger, *My Heart, Christ's Home* (Downers Grove, IL: InterVarsity Press, 1954).

This relational concept was far more influential in my mind and heart than the checklist mentality I was later taught—that is, my need to spend time with Jesus and check it off.

Oh, there is so much to learn from Jesus, my dear friend and constant companion. What a firm foundation upon which to build dreams. I am grateful. So grateful.

Out of my life story has come my journey of dreaming about, beginning, nurturing, and growing my business, Inspired to Lead. It has been a journey of ups and downs, doubts and renewed confidence. In the process, I've been called on to affirm my identity and call. Through time with the Lord, the work of the Holy Spirit, the companionship of friends and followers, the prayers of those who believed in me, and developing my skills, the journey has been an exhilarating one with known and unknown twists and turns.

One day as I was on a reading and writing week away in the Okanogan, I sat on a couch sipping lemonade. I picked up a book and began to flip through it. It was called *Inspire!*, by Lance Secretan.

As I restlessly flipped through the book, I came to this definition of inspire: "The word is derived from the Latin root word *spirare* meaning 'spirit', to breathe, to give life—the breath of God."[3]

Webster says that to inspire is like "breathing in, as in air to the lungs; to infuse with an encouraging or exalting influence; to animate; stimulation by divinity, a genius, an idea or a passion; a divine influence upon human beings."[4]

I was captured by the thought that as I look up to something or someone bigger than myself, I am enabled to receive fresh inspiration. This isn't just a nice thought. It's about having something of worth for others to be inspired by—and at that point in my life, this was quite beyond me.

I saw myself on my knees with my face lifted heavenward and my arms extended, feeling the fresh breath of God's Holy Spirit breathing new life into me. I then was able to turn to others, meet them where they were at, and breathe fresh life and encouragement into them.

---

[3] Lance Secretan, *Inspire!* (Hoboken, NJ: John Wiley and Sons, Inc., 2004), xxxii.
[4] Ibid.

Although I wasn't aware of it yet, this was the beginning of Inspired to Lead, the beginning of a wonderful journey of being invited into what God had in mind for me.

As I walked this journey, I travelled the ups of seeking to understand God's heart for me and hearing the excitement of others. I also experienced the times of my own discouragement, disappointment, second-guessing, disapproval, and condemnation. I sensed God's direction, correction, affirmation, and approval.

And although His approval of me and His invitation to me wasn't exactly the same as what we read in this passage, the principles behind it were similar.

KALEIDOSCOPE REFLECTIONS

1. Jesus heard His Father's voice speak the affirmation of His identity. What do you understand this scripture to be saying about you? How would you describe your God given identity? (See also: Psalm 139:13–16 and Ephesians 1:3–14)

    a) Write some affirmation statements that you know to be true as to how God created and formed you. Complete this statement as many times as you can in as many ways as you can: "I am…"

    b) Jot down the thoughts you read in the passages above, or other passages that are special to you. These can be passages that resonate with your heart about how you know that you are approved by God.

    c) What is a dream that He has planted in your heart that fits these affirmations?

    d) Can you think of any other passages or promptings from God through His Word, prayer, or the encouragement of others?

e) Jot down the thoughts you find yourself arguing with or resisting. Sit with them a while and observe what comes to you.

2. In what ways are you allowing God to empower you to pay attention to and use you to give truthful and challenging affirmations to others of their call from God?

3. What is your next step in being a leader who calls out God's best in others? Why does this matter?

PART ONE
FACING YOUR CRITICS

> In fact, no progress can be made toward the transformational practice of Higher Ground Leadership until we take a deep breath, centre ourselves, and resolve to be different—regardless of how much we may be criticized, how bruised our egos may become, or how dangerous it may at first appear, or how much people will tell us that persistence and metrics will suffer along the early part of the journey (which nearly always turns out to be untrue). These are all part of the necessary investment in greatness.[5]
>
> —Lance Secretan

STEPPING INTO LEADERSHIP is like putting on a red T-shirt with a big bullseye back and front. It's like saying, "Here I am. See if you can hit me. See if you can find out what's wrong with me and pound it to death."

How do we face our critics without imploding or exploding? How do we find a way that creates positive forward movement?

Feedback and criticism are two sides of the same coin. Generally speaking, when we ask for feedback, we're asking for relevant information to be given with a positive delivery. The information may not all be positive and yet the delivery is, so that we can hear it, interact with it, and use it for our own growth.

Criticism, on the flip side, is rarely anything we desire to ask for, and yet when it's given it tends to be more from a correctional or negative

---
[5] Lance Secretan, *Inspire!* (Hoboken, NJ: John Wiley and Sons, Inc., 2004), 168–169.

point of view. It often hurts and takes longer to accept and sort through. At its extreme, it can hinder our growth.

We all need feedback, since none of us know what we don't know! Feedback is necessary to help us see other perspectives and learn to bring them together for the greater good. However, criticism can diminish our sense of confidence and cause self-doubt to set in, often within seconds.

Feedback is different than criticism, and it's also different than being judgmental. We all strive to exercise good judgment, yet being judgmental generally comes from our unfiltered left brain and fires off criticism in a hurtful way. A judgmental spirit often has a lot of negative emotion attached to it, and this emotion is often the result of an uncared-for hurt in our lives.

If we have taken a leadership role of any description, we'll inevitably have faced criticism or given a judgmental comment. What we long for is feedback that affirms what is positive and gives space to hear and adapt the negative into something more positive. It allows us to turn challenges into opportunities.

Jesus faced His critics at every turn. As I considered the book of Mark through a leadership lens, I was surprised at how frequently criticism came His way.

I asked myself why I thought my experience should be any different. I wanted it to be different for me. I wanted to experience feedback without the wasted energy needed to deal with criticism and all its aftermath. After all, from my perspective, my motives are pure and in line with what my Heavenly Father asks for.

But wait—perhaps they weren't always that pure and in line with my Heavenly Father's wishes.

As I faced opportunities for growth through crushing criticism, I found the strength, comfort, and admonition to persevere, to learn and grow, to discover resilience, and to face my own ugly sense of pride. I found that I had been given an opportunity to see others and hear them in ways in which I hadn't seen or heard them before.

I remember an instance when I had a heavy conversation with a group of colleagues. I was confronted by one of them with a judgmental comment. The words spoken to me were "Wow, you sure are emotional." At the time, I straightened my shoulders and thought, *What? I didn't cry.*

Immediately I felt the reply on my lips, and it was both sarcastic and belittling: "You don't know what you're talking about."

Fortunately, I had the wisdom to take a breath before replying. Thinking quickly, I calmed myself and instead said, "If by emotional you mean passionate, then yes, I am."

This criticism led me on an interesting journey. It started out by being about trying to prove who was right and who was wrong. Over the next few meetings, however, I began to watch my colleagues display their own emotions. Some got red in the face, some got fidgety, some squirmed in their chairs, some looked down, and some became aggressive in their eye contact. In the process, I instead found myself in a place of empathy, understanding that we all have high emotion at times.

That group of colleagues was a team, created to work and collaborate together for the greater good. Although that judgmental comment started me on a negative path, it also led me to a deeper understanding of how to support my team members and how to present myself in order to better be heard.

When dealing with criticism, I face a challenge greater than myself and am given the choice to work through it. I pray that you find the grace to make that choice too.

CHAPTER ONE
THE WISDOM TO KNOW HOW, WHY, AND WHEN TO DEAL WITH YOUR CRITICS

> *When Jesus returned to Capernaum several days later, the news spread quickly that he was back home. Soon the house where he was staying was so packed with visitors that there was no more room, even outside the door. While he was preaching God's word to them, four men arrived carrying a paralyzed man on a mat. They couldn't bring him to Jesus because of the crowd, so they dug a hole through the roof above his head. Then they lowered the man on his mat, right down in front of Jesus. Seeing their faith, Jesus said to the paralyzed man, "My child, your sins are forgiven."*
>
> *But some of the teachers of religious law who were sitting there thought to themselves, "What is he saying? This is blasphemy! Only God can forgive sins!"*
>
> *Jesus knew immediately what they were thinking, so he asked them, "Why do you question this in your hearts? Is it easier to say to the paralyzed man 'Your sins are forgiven,' or 'Stand up, pick up your mat, and walk'? So I will prove to you that the Son of Man has the authority on earth to forgive sins." Then Jesus turned to the paralyzed man and said, "Stand up, pick up your mat, and go home!"*
>
> *And the man jumped up, grabbed his mat, and walked out through the stunned onlookers. They were all amazed and praised God, exclaiming, "We've never seen anything like this before!"*
>
> (Mark 2:1–12)[6]

COMING OUT OF a time of solitude, Jesus returned to Capernaum. It didn't take long for everyone to find out that He was around. The house He stayed at became so packed that there wasn't room for even one more person.

---

[6] See also Matthew 9:1–8 and Luke 5:17–26.

Some desperate people brought their paralyzed friend to see Jesus, but to get to Him they had to dig through the clay roof to lower their friend on a form of stretcher through the roof. When the stretcher and its occupant landed in front of Jesus, He immediately recognized their faith and told the man that his sins had been forgiven.

Some of the religious elite were immediately affronted and accused Jesus of blasphemy, because only God could forgive sins. Jesus challenges them on this, choosing to prove to them that He was the Son of God and could indeed forgive sins and heal this man of his leprosy. The crowd was stunned but could do nothing less than praise God.

Jesus didn't choose to get caught up in the surface issues of jealousy, power, and pettiness. He knew who He was and whose authority He carried, so He spoke clearly to the issue at hand.

At many points in my leadership journey, I have sensed the Lord impress on me the need to remain quiet, to resist jumping in to prove that I'm right. In such times, I need to buy time and remind myself that I don't know the whole story. In the ensuing quiet, my heart is calmed and my thinking becomes clearer. I come to understand that this may not be the best time to have a certain conversation, or perhaps I realize that I don't have enough information to speak intelligently.

I am reminded that I always, always have choices. Choices can move us forward or stall us in our tracks, or even move us backwards. And so I continue to learn when to speak and when to be silent.

KALEIDOSCOPE REFLECTIONS

1. How would you rate yourself in being able to recognize what the real issues are in a given situation?

2. How clear are you about where your leadership significance and authority comes from when you deal with people issues?

3. Do you ever back down from truth because it's the easy way out? Do you know why you do this? What do you need to do to change this?

4. What does it mean to submit yourself to the purposes of God as you work with people?

CHAPTER TWO
MISSING THE HEART OF THE MATTER

One Sabbath day as Jesus was walking through some grainfields, his disciples began breaking off heads of grain to eat. But the Pharisees said to Jesus, "Look, why are they breaking the law by harvesting grain on the Sabbath?"

Jesus said to them, "Haven't you ever read in the Scriptures what David did when he and his companions were hungry? He went into the house of God (during the days when Abiathar was high priest) and broke the law by eating the sacred loaves of bread that only the priests are allowed to eat. He also gave some to his companions."

Then Jesus said to them, "The Sabbath was made to meet the needs of people, and not people to meet the requirements of the Sabbath. So the Son of Man is Lord, even over the Sabbath!"

(Mark 2:23–28)[7]

ON A SIMPLE Sunday stroll, we see Jesus walking with His disciples through the fields. The disciples casually break off heads of grain, perhaps keeping the stem long to chew on as they walk.

The nearby Pharisees, of course, were prepared to have their say and criticize them: "You shouldn't be doing that! You know better than to harvest on the Sabbath!" Jesus then responds with great clarity, using an Old Testament story the Pharisees would have been all too familiar with, a story about the law having been broken for a greater purpose.

Jesus finished by confronting them out loud. He reoriented them, explaining that in the creation of the world, within the seven-day cycle

---

[7] See also Matthew 12:1–8 and Luke 6:1–5.

of life, God set aside one day to meet the needs of the people. This is called the Sabbath, and it was designed to be a day of rest and renewal, a time for people to be refreshed for the next cycle. The Sabbath wasn't designed to produce a legalistic standard for people to live up to; it was to be a day of enjoyment.

Upon first coming into leadership, I took for granted the teaching I had been raised with, that the Sabbath was a day to rest, renew, and refresh oneself. My parents' response to the Sabbath was that it was there to provide enjoyment and a time for reflection to make sense of life.

When I became a pastor, I was sure that all other pastors had been raised in the same way. I quickly learned that my perspective was just one among many. Some of my colleagues used the Sabbath to catch up on work or to get ahead for the upcoming week. For those who had preaching and teaching responsibilities on the Sabbath, they struggled with whether to take time off at some other point during the week to renew and refresh—and whether to feel guilty about it.

My appreciation for my family of origin grew as I saw all this. For me, the Sabbath provided space for me to gain perspective on life and leadership. It prepared me to handle criticism in a much healthier way, providing that moment to breathe and step back before responding.

The Sabbath is not about following a legalistic set of rules. It's about making lifegiving choices that fill and nurture us, refresh and encourage us. The Sabbath gives us space to develop a heart that is optimistic while also being realistic.

KALEIDOSCOPE REFLECTIONS

1. How would you describe Jesus's response to the false accusations of the Pharisees?

2. What other responses do you think He could have had?

3. What do you think enabled Him to choose this response?

4. What were the Pharisees missing as they criticized Jesus and the disciples?

5. Have you ever behaved like the Pharisees did in this story? Describe what that looked like for you. How did this impact the people you interacted with?

6. If you believe the heart of Jesus's explanation of the Sabbath—of it being a time of renewal and refreshment—how does that influence the way you choose to spend it?

7. Reflect for a moment on how taking this time for renewal and refreshment would enable and empower you to handle false accusations and criticism that comes your way.

8. How might your consideration of this passage influence you to develop a plan, or perhaps even a philosophy, for handling criticism?

CHAPTER THREE
LIVING BY YOUR VALUES WHEN CRITICIZED

> *Jesus went into the synagogue again and noticed a man with a deformed hand. Since it was the Sabbath, Jesus' enemies watched him closely. If he healed the man's hand, they planned to accuse him of working on the Sabbath.*
>
> *Jesus said to the man with the deformed hand, "Come and stand in front of everyone." Then he turned to his critics and asked, "Does the law permit good deeds on the Sabbath, or is it a day for doing evil? Is this a day to save life or to destroy it?" But they wouldn't answer him.*
>
> *He looked around at them angrily and was deeply saddened by their hard hearts. Then he said to the man, "Hold out your hand." So the man held out his hand, and it was restored! 6 At once the Pharisees went away and met with the supporters of Herod to plot how to kill Jesus.*
>
> (Mark 3:1–6)

WHENEVER A PERSON takes a stand for what they believe in, they provide an opening for others to agree or disagree with them. When we believe that what we say is true, and when it aligns with our values, criticism can be hard to take.

This gives us a choice. We can choose to take the comments personally and lash out, or we can choose to allow the high emotion we're experiencing bring clarity to the situation and respond in a way that is true to our character and values.

It seems that on the day written about in this passage, Jesus was in a space to rout out the critics. As He walked into the synagogue, the very first thing He noticed was a man whose hand was withered. This captured both His attention and His heart.

The story feels like a setup by His enemies, as they also saw the man with the deformed hand and wondered if Jesus would heal him. After all, it was the Sabbath. If He did, they planned to condemn Him.

Well, Jesus knew that He had come to heal the sick. So He called the man forward and gave His critics an opportunity to reveal their beliefs about healing on the Sabbath. The unbelief and brazen attempts of Jesus's critics to trap and condemn Him didn't deter Him from what He had been called to do.

Although deeply disturbed by the hardness of their hearts, Jesus didn't allow this to change His way of being or His attempts to minister to people. His critics' unbelief didn't hinder the miracles He had in store for them.

While serving in a pastoral role, I told one of my colleagues of my fear of entering a room where I didn't know what to expect or what was expected of me. What would I say? Who would talk to me? Gently, one of them reminded me that perhaps if I changed my focus, entering that room wouldn't be so daunting. He shared that He usually entered a room asking, "Lord, who needs a touch from Jesus today? Help me to recognize the need and see the person with the need."

In contrast, Jesus's enemies watched Him closely, ready to pounce. They already knew what their accusation would be if He reached out to heal the man's deformed hand. Their focus was not on what would restore and bring life, but on what would destroy and diminish, even if it brought emotional pain to a person in need of healing.

Jesus's leadership example to us is to focus on what is of most importance. He called the man forward and then, with an angry and sad heart, stepped in to give His enemies a challenge to which they had no answer.

Leadership often places a big bullseye on our backs. Are there times when you wish you could just slide under the radar instead? Yet to lead, we must be prepared and ready to handle dissent and criticism without getting bent out of shape.

KALEIDOSCOPE REFLECTIONS

1. As leaders, we receive invitations to many gatherings, not all of them in places where we're comfortable. Prior to entering any room, as a leader you wear a mantle of responsibility and privilege. Your responsibility is to represent your organization well and respect the privilege you have to serve the people there. Where is your focus as you enter a room where you've been invited? How do you prepare for the unknown?

2. What do you value most highly in your leadership? How do those values determine your outlook and behaviour when you face situations of unknown or known dissent?

3. Take a moment to jot down what you believe about unjust criticism or accusations.

4. Why is it important to know what you believe when you're caught off guard?

5. If it's difficult to articulate what you believe about how to act when you're falsely accused, try answering this question instead: how would you expect a person of character to respond? Then be that person!

6. What was of the greatest importance to Jesus in this story? Why? How do you interpret how He lived His values?

CHAPTER FOUR
FALSELY ACCUSED

One time Jesus entered a house, and the crowds began to gather again. Soon he and his disciples couldn't even find time to eat. When his family heard what was happening, they tried to take him away. "He's out of his mind," they said.

But the teachers of religious law who had arrived from Jerusalem said, "He's possessed by Satan,[a] the prince of demons. That's where he gets the power to cast out demons."

Jesus called them over and responded with an illustration. "How can Satan cast out Satan?" he asked. "A kingdom divided by civil war will collapse. Similarly, a family splintered by feuding will fall apart. And if Satan is divided and fights against himself, how can he stand? He would never survive. Let me illustrate this further. Who is powerful enough to enter the house of a strong man and plunder his goods? Only someone even stronger—someone who could tie him up and then plunder his house.

"I tell you the truth, all sin and blasphemy can be forgiven, but anyone who blasphemes the Holy Spirit will never be forgiven. This is a sin with eternal consequences." He told them this because they were saying, "He's possessed by an evil spirit."

(Mark 3:20–30)[8]

WHEN WE TAKE on the mantle of leadership, false accusations often follow. How well I remember the first sting of false accusation I received as a pastor. Through a series of events, I had pursued starting a mentoring group for young women. I had a list of approximately forty-five women

---

[8] See also Matthew 12:22–37.

who had asked to be mentored by me. Each time I was asked, I told the woman I would pray about it and put her name on the list.

When I felt I was ready to start the group, I invited twelve women to join me at my home for supper. I prepared a simple meal of spaghetti and meatballs, garlic bread, and Caesar salad. We ate while balancing plates on our laps, as I didn't have table big enough for us all.

As we gathered to chat after supper, I asked each woman to share three things with the group:

1. When did Jesus became more than a word to you?
2. What are your spiritual gifts?
3. What are you passionate about?

I cannot begin to describe the sweet spirit in the room and the powerful conversations that ensued. I invited the gals to pray about meeting once a month for supper and a spiritual conversation.

A few months into our journey together, a well-respected leader in the church approached me. This man, whom I deeply admired, told me that I was being exclusive and that it was wrong for me to pursue this. He suggested that I needed to cancel or change the group to conform to his suggestions for how it should be run.

I remember how indignant I felt, because my motives had been good. I had to make a choice—to acknowledge how I felt, face it, and figure out how to move forward with grace and truth or to be petty and small-minded, allowing myself to take it personally while hurt took root.

Through this process, I came to understand that my indignation was actually my ego crying out. This discovery felt a little like insult being added to injury—that is, until I faced my ego and pride and learned to deal with it with humility, honesty, and God's grace. I was grateful for God's grace and the love and prayers of others who guided me and led me to a healthy place.

As can only happen when God captures our hearts, this gentleman eventually became one of my most valued and much-loved mentors. And this bevy of beauties became known as Women of Influence, or

WOI. WOI has changed and morphed over the years and continues to challenge and affirm each woman involved.

Numerous passages in Mark depict religious leaders seeking to set Jesus up with their lofty accusations. In this story, Jesus is accused of getting His power from Satan.

He faced each one of these accusations, and on this occasion He used the opportunity to teach His accusers something they didn't know. His confidence in His Father's call and wisdom gave Him the courage to handle the situation well.

As we know, this didn't lead to a peaceful collaboration! What it did display, however, is that Jesus's heart was so in tune with His Father's will that He was able to work through such situations without carrying a bitter spirit—and He was able to ultimately forgive those who betrayed Him. He understood that they didn't know what they were doing.

KALEIDOSCOPE REFLECTIONS

1. As you reflect on this story, what do you think caused those closest to Jesus to think He was out of His mind?

2. Place yourself in a situation where you were falsely accused, leading to a struggle with your ego. Describe what happened and what that felt like.

3. How did you handle it? What did you learn from it?

4. In hindsight, how do you see the situation now. How has it changed you?

5. What can you learn from Christ's response?

CHAPTER FIVE
LET SILENCE DO THE HEAVY LIFTING

They took Jesus to the high priest's home where the leading priests, the elders, and the teachers of religious law had gathered. Meanwhile, Peter followed him at a distance and went right into the high priest's courtyard. There he sat with the guards, warming himself by the fire.

Inside, the leading priests and the entire high council were trying to find evidence against Jesus, so they could put him to death. But they couldn't find any. Many false witnesses spoke against him, but they contradicted each other. Finally, some men stood up and gave this false testimony: "We heard him say, 'I will destroy this Temple made with human hands, and in three days I will build another, made without human hands.'" But even then they didn't get their stories straight!

Then the high priest stood up before the others and asked Jesus, "Well, aren't you going to answer these charges? What do you have to say for yourself?" But Jesus was silent and made no reply. Then the high priest asked him, "Are you the Messiah, the Son of the Blessed One?"

Jesus said, "I am. And you will see the Son of Man seated in the place of power at God's right hand and coming on the clouds of heaven."

Then the high priest tore his clothing to show his horror and said, "Why do we need other witnesses? You have all heard his blasphemy. What is your verdict?"

"Guilty!" they all cried. "He deserves to die!"

Then some of them began to spit at him, and they blindfolded him and beat him with their fists. "Prophesy to us," they jeered. And the guards slapped him as they took him away.

(Mark 14:53–65)

WHEN WE'RE FALSELY accused, our first response is often to overtalk—that is, to speak forcefully in order to create the true picture from our perspective. Our emotions are triggered at full force and we feel the need to defend ourselves. Once we start defending ourselves, it's hard to stop.

On the other hand, silence is a ground leveller. It tends to bring words, people, and emotions to a place of reflection.

We also see this truth in a prophecy told in Isaiah 53:7. There we read that although Jesus would face oppression and be treated harshly, He wouldn't say a word. He was like a lamb led to slaughter, absolutely silent before its shearers and keeping its mouth closed.

In this story in Mark, the Pharisees tried to find evidence against Jesus to discredit Him, but they couldn't. There were false witnesses, contradicting each other.

Rather than be baited to defend himself, Jesus chose to remain silent. When Jesus did reply to a question, He was immediately pounced upon and faced fresh accusations.

We can see how Jesus responded when He chose not to defend Himself and when He chose to speak. This reveals to us that there is wisdom in knowing how to handle different situations. Knowing how to handle situations doesn't necessarily equate that everything will turn out well. We are taught that we need to understand ourselves, the situation, and the outlooks of the people we face. We can learn to see each other as equal in our creation and yet different in our being.

There are times when the most powerful and humble action we can take is to be silent. In that silence, we are given the opportunity to hear and understand before we speak.

Having a highly developed emotional intelligence also gives us an advantage, in being more self-aware and other-aware when conversations become difficult, and in understanding how to work with our self-awareness and the awareness of others to come to a place of agreement. If we can recognize how our emotions fuel our reactions, we can demonstrate effective leadership and help move the conversation in a positive direction.

Often we speak out of turn because we have emotional reactions to what others say or do. It sets off a trigger inside us. We need to learn to slow down, take a breath, and use those emotions to enrich rather than diminish the situation.

KALEIDOSCOPE REFLECTIONS

1. When faced with a difficult conversation, describe how you would differentiate the issue to be resolved and the personality and/or attitudes you might be dealing with. What does this teach us about building healthy relationships?

2. Take the time to analyze your triggers or hot buttons. What do you observe and how you can lead through the heat of them?

3. Take the time to ponder Jesus's response in the situation He faced. In the preface, we referenced the events of Mark 10:43–45 and John 13:1–17. How do you think the truths found in those passages influenced and gave Jesus the humble courage to act the way He did?

4. What observations and learnings are important to you as you think of demonstrating effective leadership while in the midst of having difficult conversations?

PART TWO
PRINCIPLES OF GROWTH

> The point to gaining knowledge is not simply learning, it is to understand and to grow both personally and professionally.[9]
>
> —Corey Olynik

THE LAW OF creation is an undisputed and unrelenting principle of growth. John expressed it this way in John 12:24: wheat kernels must be planted in the soil alone, one at a time, to die. That death will produce so many new kernels, just like a full harvest of new lives. New life out of death.

As is typical of Jesus's teaching, expectations are turned upside-down. To produce life, there is first death. To produce fruit, there is first burial. Growth then requires a lot of hard work and for us to pay close attention to the task at hand. In all we do while investing in people, a focus on growth is more important than a focus on learning and gaining knowledge.

At school, studying all manner of topics, I would whine and complain because I thought I would never use the information taught to me. Now I realize that there's so much more to learn than I ever considered.

Do you remember being a teenager? Remember your vast wealth of knowledge that exceeded anything your parents knew? And today? Don't you marvel at how little you know?

---

[9] Spoken at a teaching seminar.

Truly, knowledge opens doors of opportunity. It allows us to discover worlds beyond us. And yet knowledge on its own is not the goal; growth is. If you're a developer of people, you must grow yourself if you're going to be an effective mentor.

We can learn so much by paying attention to the rhythms of creation. Creation is like an infinity loop—from seed, seedling, plant, flower, fruit, and then back to seed. Our role is to plant, water, feed, nurture, let rest, harvest, and then take seeds and repeat the process. These are the rhythms of the life of a seed.

Sometimes in our familiarity with these processes, or maybe our casual disregard for them, they become ho-hum and we cease to appreciate the powerful truths they contain. This pertains not just to farming and gardening, but to mentoring and discipling. It pertains to how we invest in, entrust, and empower people to do the work of ministry.

In this passage, Jesus reminds His disciples that they are to plant, water, and harvest. All three tasks are everyone's job, although someone else may reap what we have sown. There is a rhythm to growth and an invitation for all to participate.

CHAPTER SIX
HOW GROWTH ORIENTED ARE YOU?

Once again Jesus began teaching by the lakeshore. A very large crowd soon gathered around him, so he got into a boat. Then he sat in the boat while all the people remained on the shore. He taught them by telling many stories in the form of parables, such as this one:

"Listen! A farmer went out to plant some seed. As he scattered it across his field, some of the seed fell on a footpath, and the birds came and ate it. Other seed fell on shallow soil with underlying rock. The seed sprouted quickly because the soil was shallow. But the plant soon wilted under the hot sun, and since it didn't have deep roots, it died. Other seed fell among thorns that grew up and choked out the tender plants so they produced no grain. Still other seeds fell on fertile soil, and they sprouted, grew, and produced a crop that was thirty, sixty, and even a hundred times as much as had been planted!" Then he said, "Anyone with ears to hear should listen and understand."

Later, when Jesus was alone with the twelve disciples and with the others who were gathered around, they asked him what the parables meant.

He replied, "You are permitted to understand the secret of the Kingdom of God. But I use parables for everything I say to outsiders, so that the Scriptures might be fulfilled: 'When they see what I do, they will learn nothing. When they hear what I say, they will not understand. Otherwise, they will turn to me and be forgiven.'"

Then Jesus said to them, "If you can't understand the meaning of this parable, how will you understand all the other parables? The farmer plants seed by taking God's word to others. The seed that fell on the footpath represents those who hear the message, only to have Satan come at once and take it away. The seed on the rocky soil represents those who hear the message and immediately receive it with joy. But since they don't have deep roots, they don't last long. They fall away as soon as they have problems or are persecuted for believing God's word. The seed that fell among the thorns represents others who hear God's word, but all too quickly the message is crowded out by the worries of this life, the lure of wealth, and the desire for other things, so no fruit is produced. And the seed that fell on good soil represents those who hear and accept God's word and produce a harvest of thirty, sixty, or even a hundred times as much as had been planted!"

(Mark 4:1–20)

SEEDS JUST ARE. They have no power of choice.

But you and I do. A seed lands in the soil either according to the plan of the planter or according to the whim of nature. From there, it either flourishes and grows or stagnates and dies depending on its environment.

Jesus unfolds this parable in sweeping strokes, at first to the crowds and then in more intimate detail to the disciples. As Jesus taught, He used parables of the familiar to help people understand the spiritual.

In explaining this parable, He expresses how He sees each group of people. Of the crowd, Jesus states that they see and do not perceive the meaning of his words. They hear and do not understand, so they will not turn from their sins and be forgiven. To the disciples, He asks a question: "If you can't understand this story, how will you understand all the other ones I am going to tell?"

We, too, get to choose. I choose by allowing the soil of my mind and heart to be receptive to the teachings of my Creator. Or I could choose to seek my own way.

Jesus is the sower who gathers the seeds and scatters them. This is quite unlike our modern way of planting in rows and planting only so many seeds per hole.

The story has caused me to reflect upon the fact that there was one sower, many similar seeds, and many different soils. I can't help but think of my personal experience of Jesus, of Him sowing His seeds of truth in me, and of me receiving them. I am the soil.

As I think back over my life, I believe there have been seasons when the soil of my mind and heart was hard and the seed was snatched away by Satan. There have been seasons when the soil was rocky; the seed landed well and yet there was no place for roots to grow, so it wilted. There have been seasons when the soil was prickly and thorny; although the seed landed and took root, it was overcome by every living thing around it. And there have been seasons when the soil was rich and fertile; the seed landed, it grew, and it produced a huge harvest.[10]

My longing is to grow, gather the seeds of Jesus's teachings, and let them take root in the soil of my mind and heart and experience growth.

Growth is evidence of the difference between knowing and being. Just gaining knowledge won't automatically translate into growth. Allowing that knowledge to transform us, to change the way we think and act, will.

In a challenging season of my life as a pastor, I came to realize that although God's truth never changes, the person in front of me comes with a unique blend of characteristics—their tendencies, personality, IQ, and emotional, mental, physical, and spiritual health and wellbeing. My role as a leader is to take the time to walk with them. I need to make space to truly come to know them and appreciate not only who they are, but also who they are becoming. In doing that, I earn the place of a trusted mentor who can pursue the give and take of the journey of growth with them and see them released into the world for ever-increasing service and ministry.

As I took on the responsibility of developing discipleship materials for our church, I had the privilege of meeting and drawing from the gifts and abilities of many skilled people. One young woman in particular came into my life, who I'll call Sue. She had been raised in a more structured and action-focused faith community than mine. She was firmly grounded in her faith.

Through a series of circumstances outside of her faith community, she came to hear about and desire to have a personal relationship with Jesus Christ. She held a high level of responsibility in her organization and was a skilled leader.

As our church began developing what it meant to establish a new believer in the Christian faith, Sue became involved with our team. It was refreshing to talk about how to do this while sitting at a table with a new believer asking us questions from her unique perspective.

I had the privilege of spending eighteen months walking through that material with Sue. We had many great discussions. We also had

---

[10] For an additional resource relating to the wisdom of the farmer, study Isaiah 28:23–29.

laughter and we had tears. There was watering to be done, weeding to be taken care of, and nurturing to pursue.

I realized that what we had written to be a thirteen-session curriculum could instead become more dynamic and living and better able to help people build a trusting relationship with each other and with God by pacing the learning with space for growth. Growth is so much more than just adding the right ingredients; it's a journey of trust, patience, perseverance, and traveling through life together.

KALEIDOSCOPE REFLECTIONS

1. Consider Jesus as a model for being a leader and teacher. How did Jesus approached this teaching opportunity? If you don't know where to start, begin by making observations using the basic questions of who, why, what, how, and where.

2. What are your observations about the processes of growth in the context of gardening, and then in the context of creating an environment for growing people?

3. What do you see as some of the broad themes in Jesus's approach to growth? Can you use these themes in your own context with growing leaders?

4. Who could you talk this over with to broaden your perspective? For example, do you know a new believer, an established believer, etc.?

5. How would you describe any shifts or affirmations in your thinking about growing people?

CHAPTER SEVEN
THE ROLE OF THE FARMER AS TEACHER

Jesus also said, "The Kingdom of God is like a farmer who scatters seed on the ground. Night and day, while he's asleep or awake, the seed sprouts and grows, but he does not understand how it happens. The earth produces the crops on its own. First a leaf blade pushes through, then the heads of wheat are formed, and finally the grain ripens. And as soon as the grain is ready, the farmer comes and harvests it with a sickle, for the harvest time has come."

(Mark 4:26–29)

JESUS WAS THE master of illustrations and could use them to make a point clear. These illustrations would create word pictures that led to Aha! moments of discernment and growth for those who heard them.

If you've ever planted a seed, then Jesus's description in this passage of a growing seed will bring memories to your mind. For those who haven't, this illustration will lack dynamism. The point of this illustration is to make the hearer think, *Been there, heard that. Let's move on to something fresh.* It could feel like old information.

As a teacher, Jesus chose to speak in ways that were relevant for His listeners. It's why some speakers focus on sports illustrations, or car illustrations, or fashion illustrations. Jesus knew His audience. He knew them because He walked with them. He did life with them. He had relationship with them. He truly listened, and He heard them.

If our endgame is to grow people, Jesus is our master teacher.

As believers, one of the major lenses through which we view life is the lens of creation. We came into existence by the purpose, plan, and loving heart of God, who created every one of us in His image.

The law of creation brings clarity to leadership development as well. In any lifegiving and dynamic pursuit, there is a created order. The farmer engages in an amazing process that he doesn't fully understand, yet he reaps the fruit of harvest as he follows those created order processes over and over again. He starts with that which is undeveloped and sees what others do not see. He sees the potential of a seemingly unimportant little seed.

The seed appears so small and insignificant, yet it holds a potential far beyond its weight or size. As the farmer works to provide what it needs for growth, the seed responds to water, sunlight, soil, manure, and the farmer's careful tending. It not only changes in size, but also in appearance and shape, becoming unrecognizable.

We have the honour of seeing potential leaders in the same way.

We're privileged to create space for these seedling leaders to grow. They are to be taken from their packages, placed in the most suitable environment, nurtured, weeded, watered, supported, and fertilized. Then we wait patiently as we journey with them.

After our budget season one year, I was given permission to advertise for an administrative assistant. I prepared the role description and distributed it for others to see. A number of applications came in and our team chose three people to interview.

And so the day began. Prior to calling in our last candidate, we reminded ourselves what we were looking for. We had already completed interviews with candidates who were self-assured and had lots of skills on paper, yet we seemed to be looking for something more.

As I welcomed our candidate into the room, she walked in determinedly and placed a red folder in front of each of the interviewers.

"I brought these with a little more information about me that you might find helpful as you make your decision," she said.

Then she sat down in a way that deferred the interview to me.

This was the beginning of a privileged season for me, as I felt right away that she was a diamond in the rough. She had a skillset and education totally different than what we had asked for, yet the way in which she attained her education had required her to use similar skills to what we were looking for. What came across throughout the interview was her character and attitude.

We hired this resourceful young woman, and there was no looking back. She applied herself and rose to every challenge thrown her way. She became one of my most valued employees and continues to be in my mentoring group today, facing every situation that comes her way with tenacity, grit, and a respect for the humanity of each person she works with.

This is one of my most cherished stories of coming to understand that growth is so much more than a program—and it illustrates what Jesus told us as a master teacher. Meet people where they're at. Walk with them. Listen to them. Hear them. Build a meaningful relationship that serves you both well. Learn the journey of leadership together.

Oh, what a privilege it is to pour into the lives of others and see them rise to their created potential. Pouring into others in this way has many nuances, large and small, and as we learn to do this we learn many lessons from the farmer who tirelessly cultivates, tends, nurtures, and harvests his crops over and over again. Jesus knew this. This is what He modelled for us, taught us, and illustrated for us.

KALEIDOSCOPE REFLECTIONS

1. If you delve into the culture and times that Jesus was called to teach in, how would you describe the way in which He used illustrations to move people's hearts?

2. Take some time to think about those you lead. What are some of their interests that could provide dynamic illustrations as you walk with them?

3. I encourage you to read Mark 4:26–29 through the lens of seeking to understand what your role is in creating space for growth. What is God's role?

4. What do you sense you most need to pay attention to as a leader who focuses on leadership development?

CHAPTER EIGHT
GROWTH IS THE MINDSET
OF A KINGDOM BUILDER

Jesus said, "How can I describe the Kingdom of God? What story should I use to illustrate it? It is like a mustard seed planted in the ground. It is the smallest of all seeds, but it becomes the largest of all garden plants; it grows long branches, and birds can make nests in its shade."

Jesus used many similar stories and illustrations to teach the people as much as they could understand. In fact, in his public ministry he never taught without using parables; but afterward, when he was alone with his disciples, he explained everything to them.

(Mark 4:30–34)

HERE WE FIND the theme of growth again. When something is repeated in scripture, it's an invitation for us to pay close attention.

In Mark 4, Jesus gives us a description of the Kingdom of Heaven, likening it to a tiny mustard seed that grows into one of the largest plants, producing long branches for birds to find shelter.

Anyone who's planted a seed, no matter how small, has had a moment where they stop in amazement at the potential of what they are putting into the ground and what they come to eventually see.

This passage shows us that creation has unstoppable rhythms that produce abundance, whether we choose to pay attention to them or not. Our role is to understand our unique creation, our call, and how we need to move from being a seed to becoming a fruit-bearer.

These ongoing rhythms of creation are the essence of Kingdom building. So often we walk the tightrope of knowing that we're called to the ministry, and sometimes we have to navigate the tension between doing what we're told, doing what others expect of us, and knowing the call of God for our lives, which involves discomfort, stretching, and often the potential for growth.

Plant, water, wait, and tend the shoots. Then water, wait, and tend the growing fruit. Then wait, harvest, and reap what was sown. Repeat! This is Kingdom building, even when it seems mundane, messy, unknown, and perhaps even insignificant. Kingdom building is about having a vision for what is to come.

The laws of creation apply to us and our ongoing growth. We need to remind ourselves of what is to be, paying attention to what produces life and weeding out what diminishes or destroys us. We are privileged to walk a very similar road with those whom we are called to influence and develop. Kingdom building starts small, as small as a mustard seed, but the journey spans from earth to heaven.

And as usual, Jesus turns our experiences and expectations on their head.

Recently, a young leader came to me with a measure of frustration over the circumstances they found themselves having to lead through. In their weariness and frustration, their focus very quickly turned. They started to wonder, *If only others in the story would shape up and be more mature.*

Knowing many of the frustrations they faced, it would be easy to side with the frustrations and in the process become part of the problem. And yet in those moments as we walk with others, our role is to hold up the photo of the fully grown garden. It's our job to remind them where they're heading, why that's important, and what that requires to get there. We must help them to take the next great step and clarify their focus.

KALEIDOSCOPE REFLECTIONS

1. Think of the scope of growth that occurs from a mustard seed to a large and productive plant. Now think of a situation you're facing as

you lead others. Where are you at in that process with someone you lead? Where are they at?

2. No matter where you see yourself today as a leader, what will it take to flourish and be productive as you lead others through a difficult season?

3. Describe what that would look like in the next week as you move forward. What do you need to know? What do you need to do? What do you need to learn?

4. Describe the bold actions you will take.

CHAPTER NINE
STORMS REVEAL OUR GROWTH
MORE THAN OUR LEARNING

As evening came, Jesus said to his disciples, "Let's cross to the other side of the lake." So they took Jesus in the boat and started out, leaving the crowds behind (although other boats followed). But soon a fierce storm came up. High waves were breaking into the boat, and it began to fill with water.

Jesus was sleeping at the back of the boat with his head on a cushion. The disciples woke him up, shouting, "Teacher, don't you care that we're going to drown?"

When Jesus woke up, he rebuked the wind and said to the waves, "Silence! Be still!" Suddenly the wind stopped, and there was a great calm. Then he asked them, "Why are you afraid? Do you still have no faith?"

The disciples were absolutely terrified. "Who is this man?" they asked each other. "Even the wind and waves obey him!"

(Mark 4:35–41)

JESUS HAD FINISHED a long day of teaching, telling stories to make a point and reach the heads and hearts of those who listened. This teaching took place outside without any sort of sound system. All He had was the strength of His voice and the ability to project it. It must have been exhausting to be constantly surrounded by people, forcing His voice to be heard.

Jesus knew His need and asked for a break to rest on the other side of the lake. He and the disciples got into a boat and began to row across.

But wait a minute. This great plan was thwarted by an ugly storm, with waves so high that they began to fill the boat with water. Unconcerned, Jesus headed to the back of the boat, found a cushion, and lay down to sleep.

All of a sudden, the terror began. Jesus woke to the sound of the disciples shouting over the roar of the storm. "Teacher, Teacher! Don't you care that we're going to drown?" With calm intentionality, Jesus, now fully awake, dealt with the storm. He commanded the wind and the waves to be silent! To be still!

I wonder, was that command for the wind and waves alone or perhaps for the disciples as well? If it wasn't for them, His next words would have held a hint of surprise, and yet no judgment. He reached out to them and asked, "What's with your fear? Do you still have no faith?"

They had walked with Him, watched Him, conversed with Him, and in the ordinary moments they had learned who He was and what He was about. Yet their first instinct was not to trust what they knew, but instead to fear.

Where was the evidence of their growth? When we're placed in a high-pressure situation, what we know becomes reality—and as leaders, we can relate. We've laid the groundwork, led the way, and yet some people doubt our leadership when difficulties come. How do we still the storm inside and out?

For a few decades now, I've spent time around the turn of each year asking God for a word or theme He might implant in my heart and mind for the coming year. I then keep that word or theme before me as I navigate the year.

One year, God gave me the concept of having *courageous humility.* As the next year unfolded, He switched it up and gave me *humble courage.* At first glance, I wondered why He was repeating Himself. As I grappled with what each concept meant for that time, I came to see how the nuance of these words fit the situations I found myself in. I found that learning and growth in a storm required both courage and humility. I discovered how easy it was to be so courageous that I lost any vestige of humility.

And I also discovered that I could too easily become subservient rather than seek to be humble and thus become ineffective. I grappled with living in the tension of humility and courage, both gifts from God.

Leading in the storm gives us the opportunity to run to the heart of God and practice everything we know so well when our worlds are calm.

KALEIDOSCOPE REFLECTIONS

1. How would you describe your initial feeling when someone questions you when things get tough?

2. Consider your heart health. In difficult situations, describe how you lead yourself through your emotions and what you focus on to be able to lead others. Is there any need to shift your focus? How could you manage that?

3. How do you tend to treat people when you feel you have prepared them and they still question you?

4. In the present situation, describe which is needed more: courageous humility or humble courage?

5. What could you learn about drawing from your inner resources that are being honed by God? How could you work with people for greater effectiveness without seeing them or their actions as the problem?

6. Describe where you envision the situation could be. Now lead.

PART THREE
LIVING BY YOUR PRIORITIES

> But you have to decide what your highest priorities are and have the courage—pleasantly, smilingly, non-apologetically, to say "no" to other things. And the way you do that is by having a bigger "yes" burning inside. The enemy of the "best" is often the "good."[11]
>
> —Stephen R. Covey

OUR PRIORITIES REFLECT what we value most, and our values determine how we make decisions and stick with them. As we seek to lead others, it becomes crucial to identify and define what we value most and how those values are reflected in our priorities.

We can see the priorities by which Jesus chose to live and the profound effect they had on His followers as well as those who sought to destroy His life and ministry. His leadership has left us a legacy today.

In my early years as a developing leader, I took a life management course from Stephen Covey. This training gave me concrete concepts and a language I could use not only with myself, but also with those whom I led.

In my role as a pastor, I found that I received many invitations to all manner of occasions and events. At first, I didn't realize that a pastor's role is public. Far more people felt like they knew me as their pastor than

---

[11] Stephen R. Covey, *The Seven Habits of Highly Effective People* (New York, NY: Simon and Schuster, 1989), 156–157.

I felt I knew them. They heard me teach and tell stories that at times revealed pieces of who I was. And so they felt like they knew me. They would invite me to baby showers, wedding showers, Tupperware parties, jewellery parties, and clothing parties.

Before I realized it, the thought of spending another evening away from home made me feel like I had a rock in the pit of my stomach. But pastors aren't allowed to disappoint others by saying no, right? My expectations of myself were unrealistic. And when I looked around at my colleagues, I saw that they, too, were on the run. Some were on stress leave.

Through avid reading and study, I came to realize that a fulfilling life would come from knowing who I was, how I was created, and what I believed. Living by my priorities became easier as I learned to understand what I valued most and based my decisions on those values and what I had been called to do.

So what about the parties and invitations?

At one point, I was asked to join a monthly clothing club. The idea was that twelve women would throw $20 in a jar every month, and each month a name would be drawn. Whoever's name was drawn would be given the full $240 to spend on clothes over the next month. Then they'd come back and model them for the gals.

That sounded fun… until I discovered that it was all church women. Now, you need to know that I love church women. And I also love so many women who don't attend church. I really value having fun, and yet I had a desire burning deep inside me to spend more time with women who didn't yet know Jesus personally.

This led me to start a different clothing club. I invited six women who loved the Lord to consider being part of it—and each of them would have to invite someone from their friendship circle who didn't know Jesus. What a fun and wonderful year we had just hanging out together!

Oh yes, the question came up: will we do devotions? No. We were just going to be ordinary women who happened to love Jesus hanging out with beautiful women who hadn't yet come to know Jesus.

Can I tell you that all those beautiful women came to know the Lord? No. But I can tell you that we learned to walk together through that year of our lives, to experience laughter, tears, and fun. We were real with each other. For those of us who knew Jesus personally, we came to allow the Holy Spirit to work in us and through us in new and fresh ways.

When we name our priorities, when we know and name the deeper desire that's burning inside, we can choose to live by those priorities and experience congruity, or an integrated life. We can experience a sense of fulfillment because this is what we were made for.

CHAPTER TEN
PERSPECTIVE IN SOLITUDE

After Jesus left the synagogue with James and John, they went to Simon and Andrew's home. Now Simon's mother-in-law was sick in bed with a high fever. They told Jesus about her right away. So he went to her bedside, took her by the hand, and helped her sit up. Then the fever left her, and she prepared a meal for them.

That evening after sunset, many sick and demon-possessed people were brought to Jesus. The whole town gathered at the door to watch. So Jesus healed many people who were sick with various diseases, and he cast out many demons. But because the demons knew who he was, he did not allow them to speak.

Before daybreak the next morning, Jesus got up and went out to an isolated place to pray. Later Simon and the others went out to find him. When they found him, they said, "Everyone is looking for you."

But Jesus replied, "We must go on to other towns as well, and I will preach to them, too. That is why I came." So he traveled throughout the region of Galilee, preaching in the synagogues and casting out demons.

A man with leprosy came and knelt in front of Jesus, begging to be healed. "If you are willing, you can heal me and make me clean," he said.

Moved with compassion, Jesus reached out and touched him. "I am willing," he said. "Be healed!" Instantly the leprosy disappeared, and the man was healed. Then Jesus sent him on his way with a stern warning: "Don't tell anyone about this. Instead, go to the priest and let him examine you. Take along the offering required in the law of Moses for those who have been healed of leprosy. This will be a public testimony that you have been cleansed."

But the man went and spread the word, proclaiming to everyone what had happened. As a result, large crowds soon surrounded Jesus, and he couldn't publicly enter a town anywhere. He had to stay out in the secluded places, but people from everywhere kept coming to him.

(Mark 1:29–45)[12]

AS WE READ these passages, we catch a glimpse of the rhythms and priorities of Jesus's life.

Right here we can put away any feelings of shame we have for not being able to figure out how to have a balanced life. Jesus didn't call us to balance; His call was to prioritize the purposes of God in a way that is true to how He created us.

As you read this passage, consider the events before and after the times of solitude Jesus pursued. Ministry has rhythms which do not equate with balance. They do equate with living by our priorities.

In this passage, after time alone with His Father, we see that:

- Jesus awoke long before daybreak.
- He got up and went alone into the wilderness.
- He prayed alone.
- His disciples looked for Him and found Him. He was together with His team.
- Once He had time with His disciples, He was ready to move on into public ministry again.
- He preached.
- He cast out demons.
- He healed the sick.

In Jesus's life, we see the power of knowing our priorities—and we can do the same as we listen to our Heavenly Father and step out to do what He asks of us. Even though the demands were great, Jesus recognized His need for solitude to reset, refresh Himself, and reaffirm who He was and what He was to do. In the midst of all the demands on Him, Jesus left to spend time with His Father. He prioritized His life and leadership, which aligned with who His Heavenly Father had created Him to be and what He had called Him to do.

---

[12] See also Matthew 26:36–44, Luke 6:12, and Luke 22:39–46.

We see Jesus living out healthy rhythms of listening to what His Father asked of Him and doing those things—preaching, teaching, performing miracles of healing, casting out demons, and pulling away from the crowds and the ministering to be alone with His Father. Jesus adapted and paid attention to His Father's wishes, Himself, others, His surroundings, and what He valued most.

As a leader, it's important to create space for times of reflection and listening. These become times of grounding and growing. By taking time to be in the presence of the Lord, God has freshened my perspective, shaped my outlook, created in me a heart that's confident in God's purposes, and led me to take actions that make a difference in the world.

I call these times God Days, and they're on my calendar in a regular rhythm. Whenever one of those days was coming, it seemed for a while that all kind of distractions showed up in my life. But once a God Day was on my calendar, I couldn't cancel it; all I could do was rebook it for another day within a two-week period. I needed that discipline to develop a healthy rhythm.

KALEIDOSCOPE REFLECTIONS

1. Consider a time when you went off by yourself to pray and spend time with God alone. What was that experience like? What was hard about it? What was a blessing?

2. Could you do it on a regular basis? Why, or why not?

3. What do you do in those moments when you're alone with God? What expectations do you take with you to that time?

4. What does that time alone do for you and your relationship with God?

5. Have you ever come back from those times feeling disappointed? If so, what was the cause of your disappointment? What did you do about that specific disappointment?

6. Do you feel that spending extended time alone with God is necessary in your life? Why, or why not?

7. What steps do you want to take to plan days like this? Will you find someone to hold you accountable for taking that time with God?

CHAPTER ELEVEN
WHAT VIEWPOINT DO YOU SEE?

Then Jesus began to tell them that the Son of Man must suffer many terrible things and be rejected by the elders, the leading priests, and the teachers of religious law. He would be killed, but three days later he would rise from the dead. As he talked about this openly with his disciples, Peter took him aside and began to reprimand him for saying such things.

Jesus turned around and looked at his disciples, then reprimanded Peter. "Get away from me, Satan!" he said. "You are seeing things merely from a human point of view, not from God's."

Then, calling the crowd to join his disciples, he said, "If any of you wants to be my follower, you must give up your own way, take up your cross, and follow me. If you try to hang on to your life, you will lose it. But if you give up your life for my sake and for the sake of the Good News, you will save it. And what do you benefit if you gain the whole world but lose your own soul? Is anything worth more than your soul? If anyone is ashamed of me and my message in these adulterous and sinful days, the Son of Man will be ashamed of that person when he returns in the glory of his Father with the holy angels."

(Mark 8:31–38)

JESUS WALKED THROUGH His life as both fully God and fully human. What must that have been like?

So often we long to know what lies ahead of us, yet as we read this passage we need to remember that Jesus did know. What would it be like to know you were going to be crucified? What would it be like to wake up every morning with that at the forefront of your mind?

Jesus eventually felt that it was time to prepare His disciples for what was to come. This wasn't pleasant news to deliver, yet He was straightforward about it.

In Matthew 16:23, we see how fully human Peter was. He didn't like what Jesus was telling them. He took Jesus aside to scold him and in return received a harsh response from Jesus. Jesus commanded him to get away from Him; He called him Satan and a dangerous trap. He accused Peter of only seeing the human perspective, not God's perspective.

Once more, we can see that Jesus's method as a leader was to point His followers not just towards the bigger picture, but also to God, the designer of the bigger picture.

We can relate to Peter's emotionally laden response, can't we? And yet we can also see the need to stop and examine how we feel. We also need to acknowledge that those feelings have the power to move us away from what truly is and what needs to be. Or they can have the power to move us closer to what could be.

Jesus remained true to what He had been called to do and what He was accountable for, despite the feelings that may have gotten stirred up in Him. This is what it means to be a servant follower of Jesus Christ.

I distinctly remember hearing my mother's voice calling me: "Ruth, have you cleaned your room and finished your chores?" I jumped off my bed as I heard my mom's voice getting ever closer to my room. It's not that I wanted to be disobedient or planned on disobeying, yet when it came to chores or dreaming, I inevitably chose dreaming. I lost sight of what was most important.

Dreaming wasn't wrong; it simply had a time and place. My mom's role was to help me recognize and lead myself to better habits. I was learning to develop healthy viewpoints in the small things of life so I would be ready for more important things when I would get to that point. My mom had a perspective I didn't understand as a child.

Similarly, Peter didn't know what viewpoint Jesus was acting from. As leaders, our perspective isn't always clear to others when we ask things of them, and yet we need to be clear in our communication and priorities.

Jesus's viewpoint was firmly set on what His Heavenly Father had asked Him to do, and He knew what He was accountable to accomplish. As you reflect on what Jesus did and who He was accountable to, consider what your viewpoint is in terms of what you do in your leadership role and who you are accountable to.

KALEIDOSCOPE REFLECTIONS

1. Take a moment to review what you have been asked to do in your leadership role and what you are accountable to accomplish.

2. Do those two concepts line up or is there something missing either in what you were asked to do and what you are actually doing? Is this the kind of accountability that moves you forward or leaves you spinning your wheels?

3. How would you address the issue and lead those whose viewpoints aren't aligned with what is expected of them and what they are accountable for?

4. What needs to shift for you to stay on track and create an empowering and accountable culture?

5. Where do you and your team need to start?

CHAPTER TWELVE
THE RHYTHMS OF PUBLIC AND PRIVATE LIFE

This is the Good News about Jesus the Messiah, the Son of God. It began just as the prophet Isaiah had written: "Look, I am sending my messenger ahead of you, and he will prepare your way. He is a voice shouting in the wilderness, 'Prepare the way for the Lord's coming! Clear the road for him!'"

This messenger was John the Baptist. He was in the wilderness and preached that people should be baptized to show that they had repented of their sins and turned to God to be forgiven. All of Judea, including all the people of Jerusalem, went out to see and hear John. And when they confessed their sins, he baptized them in the Jordan River. His clothes were woven from coarse camel hair, and he wore a leather belt around his waist. For food he ate locusts and wild honey.

John announced: "Someone is coming soon who is greater than I am—so much greater that I'm not even worthy to stoop down like a slave and untie the straps of his sandals. I baptize you with water, but he will baptize you with the Holy Spirit!"

One day Jesus came from Nazareth in Galilee, and John baptized him in the Jordan River. As Jesus came up out of the water, he saw the heavens splitting apart and the Holy Spirit descending on him like a dove. And a voice from heaven said, "You are my dearly loved Son, and you bring me great joy."

(Mark 1:1–11)[13]

SO MANY TIMES as leaders we fall into the trap of thinking we need to live a balanced life. The book of Mark is rich in stories that show Jesus choosing to go to a more private place to think and pray. Other passages

---

[13] See also Mark 1:35–39, Mark 3:13–19, Mark 6:30–44, Mark 6:45–55, Mark 8:27–30, Mark 9:1–13, Mark 9:30–32, Mark 10:32–34, and Mark 14:32–42.

tell of His need to move away from the large crowds and people who followed Him. And other times He just chose to hang out with His trusted ones.

Perhaps in your leadership role you can relate to feeling that sort of "people pressure" and wanting to go off and close your door for a moment of peace.

Perhaps you've believed the myth that leaders have all the answers, or should have all the answers, and know how to balance it all. Jesus knew that to accomplish His Father's purposes, He had to stay focused and follow the rhythms that His Father gave right from the beginning of creation.

When I come to a place of being overwhelmed, weary, and stressed, I ask myself, *What rhythm do I need to embrace in this moment?* Once those moments have passed, I ask, *What changes do I need to make in my rhythms of life?*

We often carry a God complex, needing to have it all together, but in retrospect this isn't the way Jesus ever lived, and He was capable of so much more than we are. We get into the headspace of thinking we're the only ones who can get things done, and pretty soon we feel overwhelmed. Deadlines, wanting clarity of mind, doing things right, not letting anyone down… all of these can lead us to a skewed perspective.

As I write these thoughts, I can feel the tightening of my stomach, my shoulders rising, and the fine edge of nausea I feel as I inch closer to the deadline for having to submit my strategic plans and budget for all my areas of responsibility.

While acting out of this slow-rising stress one year, a dear colleague said to me, "Who do you think you are? God?" Ouch. That stung. After all, I was only trying to get everything done, and the pressure was high.

This comment stopped me in my tracks and made me realize that I needed to step back and regroup. Quite honestly, out of my stress I wanted to hit back, yet the comment was so soul-striking that I stopped.

I don't think of that story often, but when I do I use it to conduct a self-check. What aspects of any given situation are my responsibility? Am I taking responsibility that right belongs to God or someone else? What will I do about that?

I call this "right-sizing" my life.

Our responsibility as leaders is to revisit and reflect on how God has created us, how He has called us and what we are equipped to do. These times of reflection allow us to step away from the daily demands and meet Him where He is waiting for us with challenge, encouragement, and inspiration. He made us. He knows us. He has called us by name.

Trust Him in the quiet to carry you through the chaos.

KALEIDOSCOPE REFLECTIONS

1. How would you describe the pace of your life in terms of what's going well and what feels overwhelming?

2. What in this situation is yours to own and deal with?

3. In what area(s) are you taking on responsibility that isn't yours?

4. Analyze how you allot your time and energy. For a month, track how you use your time and create categories. A simple categorization could be:
   - Name the situation.
   - What part of it is your responsibility?
   - What responsibilities do you need to ask others to complete?
   - Together, how will you accomplish what needs to be done?

5. What fills you up? What energizes you?

6. Now what? Create a simple plan to maximize your time, responsibilities, and energy rhythms. This can serve as a pattern for you when times are overwhelming.

CHAPTER THIRTEEN
FREEDOM TO CHOOSE

Then Jesus left Capernaum and went down to the region of Judea and into the area east of the Jordan River. Once again crowds gathered around him, and as usual he was teaching them.

Some Pharisees came and tried to trap him with this question: "Should a man be allowed to divorce his wife?"

Jesus answered them with a question: "What did Moses say in the law about divorce?"

"Well, he permitted it," they replied. "He said a man can give his wife a written notice of divorce and send her away."

But Jesus responded, "He wrote this commandment only as a concession to your hard hearts. But 'God made them male and female' from the beginning of creation. 'This explains why a man leaves his father and mother and is joined to his wife, and the two are united into one.' Since they are no longer two but one, let no one split apart what God has joined together."

Later, when he was alone with his disciples in the house, they brought up the subject again. He told them, "Whoever divorces his wife and marries someone else commits adultery against her. And if a woman divorces her husband and marries someone else, she commits adultery."

(Mark 10:1–12)

JESUS TAUGHT PRINCIPLES that can translate into almost any situation. Principles are enduring while methods change. Principles are what we base our decisions on; they are the basis for our freedom to choose.

In reply to a question that had been intended to trap Him, Jesus gives us a clear and factual principle—and it gave the Pharisees the privilege to decide what they would choose to do with it.

The principle: God made male and female.

The method: A man leaves his father and mother in order to be joined to his wife to become one.

As Jesus launches into the dicey topic of divorce and God's original plan for marriage, He describes the power of choice that God created humankind to exercise.

As leaders, we aren't responsible for the choices that others make. We are responsible for our own choices and the consequences they leave in their wake. We are responsible to teach clearly and compellingly the principles and truths that create space for people to grasp and embrace for themselves a satisfying and fulfilling life. It is the life God offers to us. We are to step back and ask the Holy Spirit to be the teacher and guide. We are to be ready to give an answer whenever we are asked.

But we cannot assume that God's design for life will be embraced by all, and we cannot assume that it's our responsibility to govern everyone's choices. Freedom comes in accepting self-leadership, seeking to live lives of obedience to what we know, and humbly modelling the way for others to find that same freedom.

One of the wonders of walking by faith in Jesus Christ is the power of the Holy Spirit to lead us and guide us, and allowing us to trust that He will do that for others as well. There are times when we sense that we're being set up by the questions people ask us. Our assumptions about what people know or don't know then creates frustration and can lead us to mishandle the situation.

In this passage, Jesus uses divorce as the theme around which to build His teaching, yet our focus isn't the topic of divorce. Rather, it's on how Jesus chose to handle the situation. What did He choose to do? He listened to the Pharisees' questions once again. He countered them with a question of His own that pointed them to the facts. He spoke about what they had revealed to Him regarding what they knew and didn't know.

Jesus meets people where they're at even, when they're setting Him up. I believe it was Jesus's knowledge of who sent Him, what He was called to do, and who He would one day answer to that governed His choices as He spoke to others. In this story, we see Him deliver the facts as He was given them, which also revealed how He viewed their hard hearts.

The choice to self-lead means we are given an opportunity to recognize that the situations we're in raise strong emotions in us. We can then come to a place of understanding how to recognize and handle those emotions in a way that doesn't fuel greater anger.

KALEIDOSCOPE REFLECTIONS

1. Place yourself in this same position as a leader. Crowds are gathered around you and those same voices that have questioned you before step forward and challenge you again. What kind of feeling does that create as you think about this? Complete this sentence. "If this was me, I would…"

2. Reflect on how Jesus handled the situation. Where do you think He got the strength to remain calm and factual rather than giving in to defensive feelings? What can you learn about how Jesus handled the situation?

3. Jesus was neither hostile nor meek and mild. Describe your thoughts and reflections on the tension of that stance.

4. What are you learning about yourself as a leader that would help you to be able to respond in a like manner?

CHAPTER FOURTEEN
DEVASTATION IS THE TIME TO SPEAK HOPE

As he walked away from the Temple, one of his disciples said, "Teacher, look at that stonework! Those buildings!"

Jesus said, "You're impressed by this grandiose architecture? There's not a stone in the whole works that is not going to end up in a heap of rubble."

Later, as he was sitting on Mount Olives in full view of the Temple, Peter, James, John, and Andrew got him off by himself and asked, "Tell us, when is this going to happen? What sign will we get that things are coming to a head?"

Jesus began, "Watch out for doomsday deceivers. Many leaders are going to show up with forged identities claiming, 'I'm the One.' They will deceive a lot of people. When you hear of wars and rumored wars, keep your head and don't panic. This is routine history, and no sign of the end. Nation will fight nation and ruler fight ruler, over and over. Earthquakes will occur in various places. There will be famines. But these things are nothing compared to what's coming.

"And watch out! They're going to drag you into court. And then it will go from bad to worse, dog-eat-dog, everyone at your throat because you carry my name. You're placed there as sentinels to truth. The Message has to be preached all across the world.

"When they bring you, betrayed, into court, don't worry about what you'll say. When the time comes, say what's on your heart—the Holy Spirit will make his witness in and through you.

"It's going to be brother killing brother, father killing child, children killing parents. There's no telling who will hate you because of me.

"Stay with it—that's what is required. Stay with it to the end. You won't be sorry; you'll be saved.

"But be ready to run for it when you see the monster of desecration set up where it should never be. You who can read, make sure you understand what

> I'm talking about. If you're living in Judea at the time, run for the hills; if you're working in the yard, don't go back to the house to get anything; if you're out in the field, don't go back to get your coat. Pregnant and nursing mothers will have it especially hard. Hope and pray this won't happen in the middle of winter.
>
> "These are going to be hard days—nothing like it from the time God made the world right up to the present. And there'll be nothing like it again. If he let the days of trouble run their course, nobody would make it. But because of God's chosen people, those he personally chose, he has already intervened.
>
> "If anyone tries to flag you down, calling out, 'Here's the Messiah!' or points, 'There he is!' don't fall for it. Fake Messiahs and lying preachers are going to pop up everywhere. Their impressive credentials and bewitching performances will pull the wool over the eyes of even those who ought to know better. So watch out. I've given you fair warning.
>
> "Following those hard times, Sun will fade out, moon cloud over, stars fall out of the sky, cosmic powers tremble.
>
> "And then they'll see the Son of Man enter in grand style, his Arrival filling the sky—no one will miss it! He'll dispatch the angels; they will pull in the chosen from the four winds, from pole to pole.
>
> "Take a lesson from the fig tree. From the moment you notice its buds form, the merest hint of green, you know summer's just around the corner. And so it is with you. When you see all these things, you know he is at the door. Don't take this lightly. I'm not just saying this for some future generation, but for this one, too— these things will happen. Sky and earth will wear out; my words won't wear out.
>
> "But the exact day and hour? No one knows that, not even heaven's angels, not even the Son. Only the Father. So keep a sharp lookout, for you don't know the timetable. It's like a man who takes a trip, leaving home and putting his servants in charge, each assigned a task, and commanding the gatekeeper to stand watch. So, stay at your post, watching. You have no idea when the homeowner is returning, whether evening, midnight, cockcrow, or morning. You don't want him showing up unannounced, with you asleep on the job. I say it to you, and I'm saying it to all: Stay at your post. Keep watch."
>
> (Mark 13:1–36, MSG)

SITTING IN A pew at church as a little girl with my parents, I would grip my father's hand when this story of the future was preached. The focus of course was on the devastation to come and what I needed to do if I was to get through it.

In my teen years particularly, I really focused on the fear aspect of what was to come. One example of this fear was portrayed in the movie *A Thief in the Night*. Although it also presented what it meant to find security in a relationship with Jesus, which I had, for a young teen it was a movie that nightmares are made of. This was a different time, when

TV, social media, and the news didn't hold so much influence on what we believed or didn't believe.

There were times when this passage in the book of Mark was used as a hammer to convince people to respond to the grace of God's gospel. That seemed to be an oxymoron for sure. Grace and guilt do not belong in the same sentence or paragraph!

In the story, we can see that the disciples' focus was on earthly things and that the Teacher's focus was on heavenly things! When we think back to John 13, which I wrote about back in the preface, we are reminded that Jesus knew His Heavenly Father. He knew His purpose and knew that He would be accountable for that purpose when He returned to His Heavenly Father. God the Father expressed His pleasure with His Son at His baptism before Jesus actually accomplished the work He had been sent to do. Their pleasure was in the relationship they had and the trust they had for each other. God sent Jesus to the earth with a purpose to fulfil, and when it was completed Jesus ascended into heaven to sit at the right hand of God, His Father, at a place of honour.

Jesus refocused the conversation from earthly concerns to concerns that would have not only an earthly impact but also a heavenly impact. He provided clarity in the midst of troubling and hard to understand circumstances. He also let the people know when He didn't have the information they surely wanted. Jesus focused on the facts rather than the sorts of stories that can arise when people don't have all the information they need.

And in one of the darkest passages of the future, Jesus revealed that He is the hope of the world.

Leadership can put us in a position where we want to communicate clearly, yet we may also face limitations based on confidentiality, risk management, and unknown information. Jesus recognized that His disciples couldn't handle receiving all the information they wanted at one time. As a leader, clear communication requires simplicity, careful timing, and a recognition of where your people are at. A priority from the start is to build a culture of trust and authenticity.

KALEIDOSCOPE REFLECTIONS

1. Reflect on a difficult time you faced in your role as a leader—difficult in the sense that there was only so much information for others to grasp and they wanted you to give them more. Reflect on what reactions you saw in your people. Perhaps some waited patiently and worked with what you gave them, others pushed back because they thought you were guarding secrets, and still others made up stories to fill in the gaps, which ended up creating more harm than good. In what ways did you handle the situation well and in what ways do you think you could have done things differently?

2. It's crucial to take times of reflection when challenges abound and you need to step into the gap. How do you create rhythms for reflection that keep you focused and healthy as a leader?

3. Do you relate to anyone who would be willing to keep you accountable during these times?

PART FOUR:
RISK MANAGEMENT

> Sense and deal with problems in their smallest state, before they grow bigger and become fatal.[14]
>
> —Pearl Zhu

IN TODAY'S WORLD, we have seen the tension that risk management has placed on Christian ministry. We've been challenged to address areas like social media, child protection, privacy, and lawful terminations. We grapple with how all these things work together with what we're taught in scripture.

There are times when we're afraid to address the issues in front of us, and before we know it they get blown out of proportion. We struggle with being people of grace and at times neglect the fact that truth and grace are a team for helping us address issues and move forward together. Jesus showed us the power of truth and grace working hand in hand. They are counterbalances to help us navigate conflict and risk well.

The legalism of the Old Testament is strong, clear, and concise, but it often doesn't recognize the humanity of everyone involved. It's simpler to make a clear divide between legalism and grace than do the hard work in our hearts and minds to cause them to work together for the greater good.

---

[14] Pearl Zhu, *Digitizing Boardroom: The Multifaceted Aspects of Digital Ready* (Durham, NC: Lulu.com, 2018), Kindle location 2864.

Mark poses some interesting stories that carry the potential to better understand certain risk management scenarios.

CHAPTER FIFTEEN
DINNER WITH SCUM

Then Jesus went out to the lakeshore again and taught the crowds that were coming to him. As he walked along, he saw Levi son of Alphaeus sitting at his tax collector's booth. "Follow me and be my disciple," Jesus said to him. So Levi got up and followed him.

Later, Levi invited Jesus and his disciples to his home as dinner guests, along with many tax collectors and other disreputable sinners. (There were many people of this kind among Jesus' followers.) But when the teachers of religious law who were Pharisees saw him eating with tax collectors and other sinners, they asked his disciples, "Why does he eat with such scum?"

When Jesus heard this, he told them, "Healthy people don't need a doctor—sick people do. I have come to call not those who think they are righteous, but those who know they are sinners."

(Mark 2:13–17)[15]

JESUS HAD JUST finished teaching by the lakeshore again and as He walked along, He saw Matthew at his tax collection booth. Matthew scowled as he counted his collection for the day. Would there ever be enough? Tomorrow he would up his prices.

Jesus passed nonchalantly, turned to Matthew, raised His hand in the air, and said, *"Follow me and be my disciple"* (Mark 2:14). It was a clear and simple invitation. No fanfare, no convincing, no arguing. Matthew simply got up and followed Jesus.

---

[15] See also Matthew 9:9–13 and Luke 5:27–32.

Just as casually and calmly, with a shrug of his shoulders, Matthew invited Jesus and His disciples to a banquet at his place. The dinner guests were other tax collectors and several notorious sinners.

Some Pharisees also followed as Jesus and His disciples headed towards Matthew's place. They questioned, *"Why does he eat with such scum?"* (Mark 2:16). The Pharisees' view of people didn't reflect the way Jesus saw those who needed Him. When Jesus heard that question, His response was that He hadn't come for the healthy; He'd come for the sinners, not those who thought they were already good enough.

The phrase "good enough" intrigues me. What does it mean to consider myself good enough and why would it include the sick and sinners?

Many times as I sat in board meetings, controversial topics were put on the table. I'd sense some kind of clarity around the topic in my mind and then think, *Who do you think you are to put that thought on the table? You simply aren't good enough.* I came to understand that when the focus of a thought becomes all about me rather than about the issue at hand, determining whether it's "good enough" becomes a matter of pride. In other words, Jesus once again was hitting at the Pharisees' prideful ways.

In Matthew's account of this story, Jesus challenged the Pharisees to figure this out. He wanted them to show mercy rather than demand sacrifices. He reiterated that He hadn't come to call the ones who already thought they were righteous, but rather those who knew they were sinners.

Jesus didn't call Matthew to the church. He called Him to a personal relationship with Himself, and that relationship shook and transformed Matthew's life and those he lived and worked with.

Growing up in a small town, my parents were well known for their hospitality. It spilled from their hearts, through our home and out into the streets. I remember one Sunday in particular. After the final "Amen" had been said at church, everyone gathered their belonging. The sounds of chatter began to rise.

Dad was ushering that day and had moved to the back of the sanctuary to make sure everyone had what they needed as they left. I always kept track of where he was, since he had handled some interesting situations at times.

I saw him stop and lean into the last pew. I couldn't see anyone there, yet as I got closer to Dad I noticed a rather foul odour. I pressed into him and he motioned for me to go out to the foyer. That's where I found Mom, who asked where Dad was. I pointed around into the sanctuary and she slipped over in that direction.

Mom and Dad spoke to each other for a little while, and then Mom came over and indicated that she and I would head home.

"Where's Dad?" I asked, bouncing up and down. "Aren't we waiting for him?"

She just took my hand and said that he had someone to look after.

Later that night as I was all snuggled up in bed, Mom and Dad came in to say goodnight and pray. That's when Dad explained that he had brought someone home who didn't have a home and needed some food and a bed for the night. He explained he would be late for breakfast as this new friend of his needed to get to the bus depot in the morning for a ride back to Calgary.

Half-asleep already, I reached up to give Dad a kiss. "See you in the morning," I said before turning over and diving deep under the cozy covers.

Over the years, I heard this story and many similar ones about the times my parents reached out to meet the needs of those less fortunate. In this case, the man needed food, a bed, and a ticket to get back to his family.

At times in our lives, my husband Brian and I have done the same thing, and later we watched our adult children do it too. I wasn't taught to gauge how we'd be taken out of our comfort zones for reaching out and helping others. I simply saw it lived out. I also read stories like this one in the Bible and came to understand that this is what it means to love Jesus and love others as myself.

It's not without risk, but it's also not without wisdom and love.

KALEIDOSCOPE REFLECTIONS

1. Generally speaking, how would you describe the guests you most commonly have in your home?

2. When was the last time you had someone over who was outside your comfort zone, someone who perhaps believed differently or appeared to be *lesser-than*?

3. How do Matthew's actions align with the concept of loving your neighbour as yourself?

4. What are some risks of exercising hospitality in today's culture?

5. Brainstorm some ways in which you can express hospitality to those who aren't normally in your circle of influence.

6. Why do you think Jesus put those who think they're already good enough in the same category as the sick and the sinners?

7. Have you ever felt like you were "good enough"? Did this cause you to be a better servant or a lesser servant? How did it change the way you behave or think?

CHAPTER SIXTEEN
UNDERSTANDING WINESKINS

Once when John's disciples and the Pharisees were fasting, some people came to Jesus and asked, "Why don't your disciples fast like John's disciples and the Pharisees do?"

Jesus replied, "Do wedding guests fast while celebrating with the groom? Of course not. They can't fast while the groom is with them. But someday the groom will be taken away from them, and then they will fast.

"Besides, who would patch old clothing with new cloth? For the new patch would shrink and rip away from the old cloth, leaving an even bigger tear than before.

"And no one puts new wine into old wineskins. For the wine would burst the wineskins, and the wine and the skins would both be lost. New wine calls for new wineskins."

(Mark 2:18–22)[16]

ALTHOUGH I DON'T know a lot about making and storing wine, I have a son and daughter-in-law who have mastered the art. Their wine is a delight to savour.

Wine-making is a precise art that requires much attention. If you want a quality product, it's vital to pay close attention to cleanliness to ensure that nothing foreign taints the new wine.

The context of this passage revolves around the time when Jesus was asked by the Pharisees, who were fasting, why His disciples didn't fast. In response, Jesus used the metaphor about wine and wineskins. He

---

[16] See also Matthew 9:14–17 and Luke 5:33–39.

wanted them to understand what they already knew: no one puts new wine into old wineskins. The new wine would burst the old wineskins; the wine would be lost and the skins would be ruined.

For us today, the principle is that when change happens—when something new comes along—we need to allow our hearts and minds to be open to the shifting of the Holy Spirit. This may mean letting go of old and familiar ways in order to embrace God's new and ever dynamic ways that are grounded in His principles. God cannot be contained to what makes us comfortable, and sometimes we have to let go to experience the unknown.

Our hearts can become old and brittle, prone to tearing when we focus on past ways. The past informs us in ways that allow us to build the future God has prepared for us. Our hearts remain soft and pliable to the ways of Jesus Christ when we choose to submit to His dynamic love and truth.

I've had the privilege of serving in many different capacities in organizations both as paid staff and as a volunteer. Along the way, I internalized what I've come to call "the unspoken family rules." These rules are often based on what's most comfortable to those who know them. If someone forgets they exist, there are usually consequences that seem to come out of nowhere.

I was a new hire in an established organization, excited to be doing a dream job. As a newbie, I was overeager, always pleasant, and looking to fit in. Wanting to get my office set up and get to work, I went wandering through the building's basement halls and noticed a few unused offices with furniture sitting in them. One had numerous bookcases with empty shelves.

Without thought of the potential consequences, I naively wrangled two of these bookcases and brought them up to my office. Ah, lovely!

In short order, I found myself face to face with a team leader, who informed me firmly that no one moved furniture without his permission and that the bookcases were to be moved back. The physical exertion required for me to move those heavy, awkward bookcases back to their original spots worked to dimmish some of the stress I felt.

In this case, a new wineskin (me) was creating stress for an old wineskin (the team lead). Fortunately, we were able to discuss the situation and came to an acceptable solution for each of us without letting petty hurts get in the way.

Jesus knew when to address the situation and when to consider the need for new wineskins to move forward.

KALEIDOSCOPE REFLECTIONS

1. Describe your calling, as you understand it.

2. Although Jesus had the most crucial calling while He was on the earth, why do you think He was so approachable? Define Jesus's calling.

3. What was the lesson He was trying to get across with His example of the wineskins?

4. What causes your heart to become rigid and unpliable? How approachable are you when that happens?

5. What do you intentionally do to keep your heart soft and pliable to God's truths?

6. What is one truth He has given you lately that was a struggle for you to accept? What are you doing about it? How can you use it to encourage others?

CHAPTER SEVENTEEN
PREPARED TO BALANCE MINISTRY AND POWER

> *Jesus went out to the lake with his disciples, and a large crowd followed him. They came from all over Galilee, Judea, Jerusalem, Idumea, from east of the Jordan River, and even from as far north as Tyre and Sidon. The news about his miracles had spread far and wide, and vast numbers of people came to see him.*
>
> *Jesus instructed his disciples to have a boat ready so the crowd would not crush him. He had healed many people that day, so all the sick people eagerly pushed forward to touch him. And whenever those possessed by evil spirits caught sight of him, the spirits would throw them to the ground in front of him shrieking, "You are the Son of God!" But Jesus sternly commanded the spirits not to reveal who he was.*
>
> (Mark 3:7–12)[17]

IN A PREVIOUS passage, Jesus experienced a number of emotions in the midst of His ministry on the Sabbath. He felt angry, sad, and deeply disturbed. Yet the story reflects the power struggle that was present. Jesus's clarity around what He was to do on behalf of His Father meant that He continued to preach, teach, and heal despite the criticism He received. He refused to enter the power struggle.

Perhaps this is what we would consider a day in the life of Jesus. He and His disciples went out to the lake, followed by a huge crowd from all over Galilee, Judea, Jerusalem, Idumea, from east of the Jordan River, and from as far away as Tyre and Sidon. The news about His

---
[17] See also Matthew 12:15–21.

miracles had spread far and wide, and people who came to see Him for themselves lined up as far as could be seen.

Jesus, in His foresight, asked the disciples to bring a boat and have it ready in case He got crowded off the beach.

There had been many healings that day, which drew a crowd of many sick people who wanted to touch Him. When those possessed by evil spirits caught sight of Him, they threw themselves in front of Him and shrieked, "You are the Son of God!"

In the previous passage, after Jesus healed a man on the Sabbath the Pharisees headed out to plot His death. As time went on, the crowds got bigger and more passionate. It would have been easy to focus on the crowds, on the numerical increase of His work and the powerful sway He was obviously having. And yet Jesus moved in and among the people and kept His heart, mind, and eyes clearly on the reason why He was there. His heart was to achieve His Father's purposes.

When power and emotions are in play, it's easy to lose our focus. In times of reflection, we gain fresh knowledge, wisdom, and strength to keep ourselves firmly focused on what's of most importance and not give in to the strength of our emotions and the power struggle within and around us.

As a young Bible college student, I had the privilege of traveling with a concert choir. After hours and days and weeks of practicing and seeking to learn the music, our heads were pretty full of what we needed to do. It was easy to nervously focus on the technical correctness of the performance, yet our director, who was a pretty good taskmaster, encouraged us to take a step back and be reminded of why we were doing this. He wanted us to rest in the work of the Holy Spirit, who could take the words and music and use them to glorify God and edify the people present, including ourselves.

I will never forget one night when the director led us in prayer. He prayed that God would take all that we offered to honour Him, even our mistakes.

What? Mistakes? We had been drilled to get it right. In fact, I had come to think that getting it right was the only way God would be able to work through us.

Oh, what a faulty conclusion that was. I came to learn that God works not in our rightness, but in our submission to His love and purposes. And yes, sometimes He even uses our mistakes! How freeing it was to let God be God and simply and profoundly live in obedience to Him.

KALEIDOSCOPE REFLECTIONS

1. How would you describe the term "ministry"?

2. What is your definition of the term "power"?

3. What is the difference between these two terms?

4. Have you seen either of them misused?

5. What role do they play in the life of a leader?

6. Have you ever mixed the two up? If so, describe the situation.

7. What could you have done differently?

8. How would you help an emerging leader understand the difference?

CHAPTER EIGHTEEN
WHAT DO PIGS HAVE TO DO WITH RISK MANAGEMENT?

So they arrived at the other side of the lake, in the region of the Gerasenes. When Jesus climbed out of the boat, a man possessed by an evil spirit came out from the tombs to meet him. This man lived in the burial caves and could no longer be restrained, even with a chain. Whenever he was put into chains and shackles—as he often was—he snapped the chains from his wrists and smashed the shackles. No one was strong enough to subdue him. Day and night he wandered among the burial caves and in the hills, howling and cutting himself with sharp stones.

When Jesus was still some distance away, the man saw him, ran to meet him, and bowed low before him. With a shriek, he screamed, "Why are you interfering with me, Jesus, Son of the Most High God? In the name of God, I beg you, don't torture me!" For Jesus had already said to the spirit, "Come out of the man, you evil spirit."

Then Jesus demanded, "What is your name?"

And he replied, "My name is Legion, because there are many of us inside this man." Then the evil spirits begged him again and again not to send them to some distant place.

There happened to be a large herd of pigs feeding on the hillside nearby. "Send us into those pigs," the spirits begged. "Let us enter them."

So Jesus gave them permission. The evil spirits came out of the man and entered the pigs, and the entire herd of about 2,000 pigs plunged down the steep hillside into the lake and drowned in the water.

The herdsmen fled to the nearby town and the surrounding countryside, spreading the news as they ran. People rushed out to see what had happened. A crowd soon gathered around Jesus, and they saw the man who had been possessed by the legion of demons. He was sitting there fully clothed and perfectly sane, and they were all afraid. Then those who had seen what happened told the others about

> the demon-possessed man and the pigs. And the crowd began pleading with Jesus to go away and leave them alone.
>
> As Jesus was getting into the boat, the man who had been demon possessed begged to go with him. But Jesus said, "No, go home to your family, and tell them everything the Lord has done for you and how merciful he has been." So the man started off to visit the Ten Towns of that region and began to proclaim the great things Jesus had done for him; and everyone was amazed at what he told them.
>
> (Mark 5:1–20)

IN THE LAST number of decades, risk management has added great complexity to ministry. A simple way to understand risk management is to grasp the purpose behind it: to identify potential problems and put mitigating factors in place to reduce the potential for adverse costs to the organization. These costs are measured in the expenditure of finances, people, time, energy, and facilities.

One example of risk management in our world today concerns the effects of mental illness. We often see the law being used to try to mitigate these risks.

In this passage, we encounter a man who perhaps suffered not only from a form of mental illness but was also possessed by evil. Jesus chose to deal with the evil in His midst first, and because of His deep faith and spirituality it stood out as His most pressing priority.

As I read this passage through leadership eyes, I remembered numerous conversations I've had around the leadership table. A simple example is summer camp. When I went to camp as a kid, we would go horseback riding. This was usually made possible because the neighbours had a horse or two that the camp could rent. The camp fees were low back then because insurance usually didn't address such activities.

Later, as a junior counsellor, I was entrusted with teaching riflery even though prior to camp that year I had never held a rifle. I received the minimal training and certainly never signed any waivers.

Today, risk is a much more significant cost.

As I read about how Jesus sent the evil spirits into the pigs, I wondered about the owner of those pigs. What were his losses? Who was going to have to clean up after Jesus's choices? What did it cost as two thousand pigs ran over the hill, fell into the lake, and drowned?

Every choice we make creates a wake behind us. That wake can create greater momentum, or it can create harm and even destruction. In risk management, we must ask ourselves, *If I choose this action, what will it cost?* The question goes beyond finances; it concerns the cost of time, energy, people, facilities, and ultimately even personal cost.

As is common in the Gospels, we aren't privy to the whole story regarding the pigs. One conclusion we can draw is that Jesus knew His priorities and was prepared to address the consequences of His actions in ways that honoured His Father and His call.

Even as the herdsmen ran to tell others what had happened and people came to se the possessed man clothed and in his right mind, they were moved by fear, not by faith. The crowds begged Jesus to go away.

As Jesus climbed into the boat to leave, the man asked to go with Jesus. His fear had been addressed and now he had faith. Jesus had saved him from certain death and given him the opportunity to choose life.

As he went on his way, this man was empowered to tell his story and bear witness to the life-changing power of Jesus.

KALEIDOSCOPE REFLECTIONS

1. As you ponder this story, what do you learn about the priorities that guided Jesus's way with people?

2. How can you embrace those same priorities, even if they look different today than in how Jesus lived them out?

3. Risk management has changed the operations of ministry. At times it requires us to address long-neglected issues. At other times, it seems to interfere with the work of the Lord. Reflect on how risk management has changed the operations of your ministry. We all need to understand what triggers us and gives us the opportunity to react or respond. Reflect on what would allow you to become a responder rather than a reactor when those triggers go off. Jot down and name your personal and ministry values, fleshing out how to live by your values even when you're challenged, all the while keeping Christ's love at the forefront.

4. Are you experiencing any frustration that could lead to un-Christ-like attitudes or behaviours like blame, shame, judgment, etc.? What is the next step you need to take to remain true to your call?

PART FIVE
RELATIONAL WEALTH

> Our lives succeed or fail gradually, then suddenly, one conversation at a time. While no single conversation is guaranteed to change the trajectory of a career, a business, a marriage or a life, any single conversation can. The conversation is the relationship.[18]
>
> —Susan Scott

RIGHT FROM GENESIS 1, we quickly recognize that the heart and mind of the Father was to create us for community and relationship. And yet I've heard many leaders say in moments of relational frustration, "If I could only focus on ministry and not have to deal with people, life would be good."

As we watch Jesus, we realize that there is no ministry without people, and therein we face one of our greatest tensions. Jesus met people where they were at and invited them into something so much more than what they were experiencing. In John 13, Jesus demonstrated grace, character, and truth in kneeling to wash the feet of the one who was to betray Him.

I've also experienced this grace through foot-washing. While completing my year of teaching Career and Life Management to a small senior high school class, I became overwhelmed. When graduation day arrived, it came with a mix of beauty, excitement, giggles, tears, sadness, and hope.

---

[18] Susan Scott, *Fierce Conversations* (New York, NY: Penguin Group, 2002), viii.

As I entered the school foyer and moved through to the gymnasium that day, I felt a little off-balance. My attention was drawn in many directions. The gymnasium had been transformed into a wonderland—except for the lingering aroma of sweaty gym wear by the change room doors.

I heard my name repeatedly as students wanted to show me what they had helped to create. As I witnessed their beauty, youth, and energy—all of them dressed in their very best—I felt a lump in my chest. My throat caught and tears pressed from my eyes and ran down my cheeks. I just wanted to hold this moment in time. Where would they all end up? What would they face as they entered adulthood?

As I gazed around the room, I noticed a circle of chairs draped with towels on their backs. Bowls had been placed in front of each chair. While taking it all in, one of my students, a young man named Trevor, came over and asked to escort me to one of the chairs. He explained that the students wanted to wash the teachers' feet as a gift of gratitude for all we had invested in them that year.

I had a deep appreciation for what was about to happen. But no one had ever washed my feet before, making this a new and not entirely comfortable experience. Oh yes, I knew the passage about Jesus washing the disciples' feet, but in real life it seemed different. I felt a little flustered, all hot and cold.

The fact of the matter is that I had worn nylons. I didn't want to ruin this moment, but what was I to do about it? Calmly, I excused myself to slip into the washroom. I leaned on the cubicle door, took in a big gulp of air, then removed my nylons and stuffed them in my purse. Afterward, I exited to the gymnasium and sat on my designated chair.

Enter the holy moment.

The teacher who represented the grad class rose and asked for everyone's attention. "Today our grads want to express in a tangible and servant-hearted way how much each of you has meant to them this year," the teacher began. "As I read from John 13, they will wash your feet as an expression of gratitude to you and for your investment."

I truly can't describe how I felt as Trevor gently picked up one of my feet and placed it in the basin of water, rinsed it, and lowered it on the towel across his knee. I felt humbled and hesitant as I tried to move beyond the discomfort.

As he began to wash my other foot, I focused on his head bowed before me. I asked God to draw him close to His heart, meet him where he was, and provide for and protect him in all ways.

What a privilege it had been for me to spend my time with such great kids. Oh yes, they tested me, and oh yes, they blessed me. In our final experience together, we were united through the humility and respect. We followed the example of Jesus, who spoke often about community, relationship, and what it means to serve one another.

CHAPTER NINETEEN
WHO IS MY FAMILY?

Then Jesus' mother and brothers came to see him. They stood outside and sent word for him to come out and talk with them. There was a crowd sitting around Jesus, and someone said, "Your mother and your brothers are outside asking for you."
Jesus replied, "Who is my mother? Who are my brothers?" Then he looked at those around him and said, "Look, these are my mother and brothers. Anyone who does God's will is my brother and sister and mother."

(Mark 3:31–35)[19]

AS JESUS ENTERS the discussion and speaks to the definition of a family, He brings clarity to the messiness of life. We like to organize where everything and everyone fit. Jesus tips those boxes on edge and challenges our thinking.

In this instance, He wants us to think about who we consider our family to be. It's no longer as simple as who's in our bloodline. Jesus broadens the scope to include those who do God's will.

This leads me to a common type of conversation that comes up time and time again as we try to organize and make life clear-cut and simple. What does it mean to find balance between all my competing opportunities and relationships? Perhaps the degree of separation is not so great as we think. Perhaps the same principle applies in our broader search for a work-life balance.

---

[19] See also Matthew 12:46–50 and Luke 8:19–21.

Many people are crushed and defeated as they seek to live perfect lives, achieving the perfect work-life balance, only to find that this isn't what God ever intended.

As I served my boss and colleagues in retail for ten years in a management role, and then later as I served my staff, volunteers, and congregants in the church for thirteen years, I grappled with the concept of achieving work-life balance, something which I heard about time and again. It was a pretty common conversation around the watercooler.

In wrestling with this idea, I felt drawn to look at the life of Jesus and how He handled His work-life balance. I was amazed, almost giddy, as I discovered that rather than seeking a balanced life, Jesus had a rhythm to His life.

God called us and gifted us to go about His business, to show the world what it looks like to have Jesus by our side, to pave the way for others to come to a personal relationship with and live wholeheartedly for Him.

We need to understand that whatever is a part of our lives—whether it be family, career, sports, friendships, food, or entertainment—comes with an opportunity to live with Christ at the centre of each part of our lives. We can live in the shifting tension that comes from realizing that different things will be most important to us depending on the situation. There are no simple rules or formulas to avoid bump-ups and collisions, yet choices abound when it comes to our attitude and actions.

In this passage, Jesus addresses His views on family. His mother and brothers arrived at the house where He was teaching. They stayed outside and sent a message to let Him know they were there and ask Him to come and talk with them. Jesus was surrounded by a crowd when someone in the crowd told Him, "Your mother and brothers and sisters are outside asking for You."

Jesus's reply may be disconcerting. He asks who His mother and brothers are. As His gaze sweeps across the crowd, He says that the people in front Him are His mother and brothers. He then clarified that anyone who chooses to do God's will is His brother and sister and mother.

As you think of Jesus's response, you may feel a sense of confusion or clarity around what it means to have a work-life balance. There is confusion because Jesus extends the definition of family beyond the traditional definition. If you associate having a family with a life that equally weighs everything in it, it becomes really unclear as to how balance can be created between home and work. If you think of living life according to a rhythm, you can gain greater freedom and clarity on how to make decisions.

KALEIDOSCOPE REFLECTIONS

1. How do you define family?

2. What is your response to this passage, and why do you respond that way?

3. Consider Romans 8:12–17. What does it look like to be a member of God's family? List the benefits.

4. The church often refers to itself as a family. What does that look like for you personally?

5. What are the challenges we face as a church family?

6. What is the responsibility of the church to provide a sense of family for those who attend?

7. What is your responsibility to provide a sense of family in your area of ministry?

CHAPTER TWENTY
KNOW WHEN TO WALK AWAY

When the Pharisees heard that Jesus had arrived, they came and started to argue with him. Testing him, they demanded that he show them a miraculous sign from heaven to prove his authority.

When he heard this, he sighed deeply in his spirit and said, "Why do these people keep demanding a miraculous sign? I tell you the truth, I will not give this generation any such sign." So he got back into the boat and left them, and he crossed to the other side of the lake.

(Mark 8:11–13)

THESE THREE VERSES cut to the essence of the relationship Jesus had with the Pharisees. Picture this: Jesus had just finished healing a deaf man and was facing crowds of people. He also had fed the four thousand and cleaned up before getting into a boat with His disciples to go to the region of Dalmanutha. He'd spent a full day facing thousands of people and performing amazing miracles.

And then as He arrived in Dalmanutha, the Pharisees were waiting to bait Him, to test Him and try and to start an argument.

In verse 12, we can observe His actions:

1. He listened.
2. He took a deep breath in His Spirit.
3. He replied concisely.
4. He left.

That's all we get. Think about the progression of how Jesus handled this situation, which held the potential for great conflict and heated words that couldn't be taken back.

These four points give us a framework for how to react when tensions and emotions are high and we feel triggered. We all know that feeling: our gut tightens, our neck gets stiff, our shoulders rise, we swallow, our heart races, our fists clench, our face begins to feel warmer... We want to straighten everything out right away. You could say we are reactionary.

Jesus didn't react. He responded. He didn't ignore the situation or the heat of it, but He took the time to lower the temperature and make sure the environment was one in which He could be heard. Then he let the Pharisees have the freedom to choose their next step.

KALEIDOSCOPE REFLECTIONS

1. Revisit a touchy situation you've faced, or one you're currently facing. How would these four concepts work for you to enable you to move from being reactionary to responsive?

2. What does practicing these four concepts look like in your present situation?

3. As a leader, what triggers your emotions and causes you to react rather than respond?

4. How might you adopt this four-point response the next time you face hostility, accusations, or unfair judgments?

5. Who will you choose to walk with you in learning to respond more often than you react?

CHAPTER TWENTY-ONE
PERCEPTION VERSUS REALITY

Jesus and his disciples left Galilee and went up to the villages near Caesarea Philippi. As they were walking along, he asked them, "Who do people say I am?"

"Well," they replied, "some say John the Baptist, some say Elijah, and others say you are one of the other prophets."

Then he asked them, "But who do you say I am?"

Peter replied, "You are the Messiah."

But Jesus warned them not to tell anyone about him.

(Mark 8:27–30)[20]

IN MARK 8, Jesus was concerned about the perception others had of Him. This doesn't naturally equate with whether people liked Him. When we remember John 13, we can see that Jesus knew His purpose, who sent Him, and who He was to return to. We can grasp that this was more about understanding the wake He left behind than about Himself and His ministry.

Whether we intend to or not, we all leave a wake behind us. Those wakes can be positive or they can be destructive.

As I was heading off to a speaking engagement one day, settling into my seat on a full flight, a woman unintentionally bumped my arm while heading to the washroom at the front of the plane. We acknowledged each other with smiles. There was no problem.

---

[20] See also Mark 10:32–34.

Just as the stewardess was asking everyone to check their seatbelts, I looked up to see this same women heading back to her seat. As she approached, I noticed to my horror that she had a piece of toilet paper hanging from the waistband of her jeans. I made a split-second decision, then gently touched her arm to motion her to bend over to hear me.

"Please don't react quickly," I said, "but there's a piece of toilet paper stuck in your waistband and hanging down."

I held her arm, wanting to prevent her from drawing any more attention than necessary. She slowly reached behind herself and pulled the toilet paper away. She then crumpled it up and went to her seat.

Once we were in the air, she came back to my seat, leaned on the armrest, and said, "Thank you so much, I had no idea. That could have been so much more embarrassing! Thank you for your graciousness."

Out of an embarrassing situation, we both gained a new acquaintance.

This story often comes to my mind when I think of how important it is to check the wake we leave behind us.

As leaders, we can become caught up in the vision we're casting and moving people towards—and that can be empowering. We're also to be aware of what we leave behind us. Whatever the wake we leave, we are responsible to lead through it and manage it.

Jesus was checking His wake in this passage, and He ends with a strange warning to His disciples. He had just heard about the mixed concepts people had about Him and knew that His disciples saw clearly who He was. But He warned them not to tell anyone about Him.

As leaders, we often perceive that we need to defend the way things are, or defend someone else. Sometimes we even feel the need to defend God. And yet knowing our beliefs, values, and purpose, there are times when our actions speak most powerfully.

Jesus needed no defence. He knew who He was and what He was to be about. He knew His Father and that His Father had His back. He knew the road ahead, and He knew why that road was the one He had to walk, no matter what anyone thought. He had a higher purpose, a clear empowerment and accountability. His perception of reality was weighted in who He was and what He had been called to do.

KALEIDOSCOPE REFLECTIONS

1. Read these two passages a few times and let them wash over you. What do you sense the Holy Spirit impressing on your heart?

2. How does this impression by the Holy Spirit tie in with what you know to be your purpose, empowerment, and accountability? Record these and express why they're so important to accomplishing what you've been called to do.

3. How do you pass the importance of this concept on to those you have the privilege and responsibility to lead?

CHAPTER TWENTY-TWO
CHILDLIKE, NOT CHILDISH

> *One day some parents brought their children to Jesus so he could touch and bless them. But the disciples scolded the parents for bothering him.*
>
> *When Jesus saw what was happening, he was angry with his disciples. He said to them, "Let the children come to me. Don't stop them! For the Kingdom of God belongs to those who are like these children. I tell you the truth, anyone who doesn't receive the Kingdom of God like a child will never enter it." Then he took the children in his arms and placed his hands on their heads and blessed them.*
>
> (Mark 10:13–16)

THE WORD "CHILDLIKE" brings to mind a picture of sweetness, openness, wonder, and innocence. You may see the face of a child who at times drives you crazy with all their whys, yet they're forming their values and their questions come from a place of curiosity and understanding.

One day as my husband Brian and I were leaving on a walk, we stopped to catch up with our neighbour. Her little son ran over and said, "Ruth, why do you guys go for a walk every day?"

His mom quickly answered, "They enjoy walking like you enjoy riding your bike."

"Oh," he replied. And off he ran to get his bike.

Simple question, simple answer, and on to the next thing.

The word "childish," by contrast, creates another picture, this one of demanding and tiring behaviour. The picture we hold in our minds is usually one of selfishness and whining, even tantrums when pushed to the extreme.

Being childish is a part of childhood, as we learn to understand and navigate our emotional responses. In 1 Corinthians 13, we are reminded that when we become adults, we put away our childish ways.

As a leader reading this, does childishness not just make you weary?

Jesus saw the beauty and potential in a childlike heart, eyes and heart wide open to see and learn and grow.

Although the disciples meant well when they saw the parents bringing their children to Jesus, their action to remove the children from bothering Jesus didn't align with His heart for the children. The Pharisees acted from their perspective, yet Jesus saw something very different. He saw the innocence and purity of a child's heart and knew this was the kind of heart that was needed to receive the Kingdom of Heaven—a childlike heart, full of innocence, anticipation, and wonder.

This kind of heart is anything but childish. Jesus, although fully God and fully man, had this kind of childlike heart and faith as He related to His Father and to those around Him.

Having a childlike heart doesn't equate to lacking knowledge or a backbone. A person with a childlike heart has the ability to hold knowledge and perspective without judgment or condemnation of others.

KALEIDOSCOPE REFLECTIONS

1. Take a moment to think about your reactions (that can be childish) or your responses (that can be childlike) to others, especially when there's a difference of opinion or perspective.

2. Can you name the emotions you feel when you have a tendency to react childishly?

3. Can you name the emotions you feel when you're prepared to respond in a childlike way?

4. Reflect on what's different between these two and how you can become more self-aware as a leader.

5. How can you influence the people you lead to become better aware of how their emotions determine the course of a conversation?

6. How will you allow these concepts to free you to understand your responses with greater clarity and respond accordingly?

CHAPTER TWENTY-THREE
A BEAUTIFUL PATTERN FOR FAREWELL

On the first day of the Festival of Unleavened Bread, when the Passover lamb is sacrificed, Jesus' disciples asked him, "Where do you want us to go to prepare the Passover meal for you?"

So Jesus sent two of them into Jerusalem with these instructions: "As you go into the city, a man carrying a pitcher of water will meet you. Follow him. At the house he enters, say to the owner, 'The Teacher asks: Where is the guest room where I can eat the Passover meal with my disciples?' He will take you upstairs to a large room that is already set up. That is where you should prepare our meal." So the two disciples went into the city and found everything just as Jesus had said, and they prepared the Passover meal there.

In the evening Jesus arrived with the Twelve. As they were at the table eating, Jesus said, "I tell you the truth, one of you eating with me here will betray me."

Greatly distressed, each one asked in turn, "Am I the one?"

He replied, "It is one of you twelve who is eating from this bowl with me. For the Son of Man must die, as the Scriptures declared long ago. But how terrible it will be for the one who betrays him. It would be far better for that man if he had never been born!"

As they were eating, Jesus took some bread and blessed it. Then he broke it in pieces and gave it to the disciples, saying, "Take it, for this is my body."

And he took a cup of wine and gave thanks to God for it. He gave it to them, and they all drank from it. And he said to them, "This is my blood, which confirms the covenant between God and his people. It is poured out as a sacrifice for many. I tell you the truth, I will not drink wine again until the day I drink it new in the Kingdom of God."

Then they sang a hymn and went out to the Mount of Olives.

(Mark 14:12–26)

IN THIS PASSAGE, we're given a beautiful example for saying farewell. Generally speaking, when we arrive at a destination we are greeted, introduced, and feel a sense of belonging. As time goes by, it becomes important to consider how to say goodbye in a way that contributes to ongoing trust for ourselves and for the organization we're leaving. It's all too common for staff or volunteers to just not be there anymore. This creates distrust.

Goodbyes are as important as hellos. We know that when we bring someone new into a setting, we pave the way for them to be received and even welcomed. When someone leaves an organization, the same applies. We have the opportunity to create new levels of trust by the way we let someone go or by the way we treat them when they choose to leave.

Thinking through how you intend to leave is just as important as thinking through how you intend to enter a relationship or organization. Jesus entered our world as innocent and sweet as a helpless baby. He left this world betrayed and crucified. After His resurrection, He ascended to sit at the right hand of His Father in heaven as a mature and knowing leader, receiving the approval of His Father.

Going back to the passage, which we often refer to as the Last Supper, we see that Jesus knew the hearts of those at the table. He still chose to eat with them, to let them know He was aware of what was to come, and to wash their feet.

And so, as Jesus prepared to leave this earth, He gave us a beautiful example to follow:

1. He knew the space He wanted for this final gathering and made sure it was reserved for Himself and the disciples.
2. He gathered His disciples with Him around the Passover table. They broke bread.
3. He led them in a time of communion, which was to be their comfort and strength once He returned to His Father.
4. They sang a hymn together.
5. They prayed together.
6. They went out together.

Can you imagine the intensity? The emotional highs and lows? The questions and doubts? The fears and certainties? All of that for the leader who was leaving, as well as for those who would remain. It was a vortex of emotional and mental strain. Jesus knew He would see these loved ones again and that leaving in a healthy way would create space for a wonderful reunion one day.

I haven't always left well, and yet I have aimed to leave in a way so that I would never be embarrassed to be with people should I see them again.

I worked at a little quilt store for nine years. I was the co-manager entrusted with the people side of the business. At that time, there were twenty-two part-time employees. We had a great staff and staff environment. Expectations were clear and accountability was as simple as having a conversation.

But a situation arose with one employee that needed to be addressed. When I was made aware of the issue, it created angst for me. I knew this employee was dearly loved by the owner and was known for her talent. With trepidation, I arranged to sit down with the owner and we made a plan to meet with the employee.

The meeting took place one day after the store was closed. This was one of my first opportunities to learn that no matter how well I prepared to handle a situation well, there is always more than one perspective to consider—and every perspective has a human heart behind it. The conversation we had that day was difficult.

When this employee eventually moved on from the job, I realized that celebrating farewells is crucial in order for everyone to experience healthy closure and to know that no matter how many differences people have they can say goodbye well and move on. It allows people to cross paths again without having to avoid each other.

Never burn your bridges, as you never know when you'll need to walk over them again.

So many times I continue to cross paths with people who I've said goodbye to, and often at that moment of goodbye I never thought I would see them again. And yet I have.

I long to continually learn to walk with a free heart, whether it be in hellos or goodbyes.

KALEIDOSCOPE REFLECTIONS

1. Have you ever considered what it would be like to leave an organization when everything isn't in order, when tensions are high, disagreements unsettled, and accusations unfair? Take some time to think about what it would take to leave well with no unfinished business.

2. What would be some of the priorities or values you would lean into to guide you and keep you on the high road?

3. What does it mean to not burn your bridges, and what does this look like in real life?

4. Review the six things Jesus did to prepare for the Last Supper. How can they guide your responses and keep you from reacting in a negative way? Go through each point to see what value it contains to help you to move forward in a positive way.

5. What kind of outside accountability would be a strength and encouragement to you?

CHAPTER TWENTY-FOUR
THE POWER TO SPEAK TRUTH

On the way, Jesus told them, "All of you will desert me. For the Scriptures say, 'God will strike the Shepherd, and the sheep will be scattered.' But after I am raised from the dead, I will go ahead of you to Galilee and meet you there."
Peter said to him, "Even if everyone else deserts you, I never will."
Jesus replied, "I tell you the truth, Peter—this very night, before the rooster crows twice, you will deny three times that you even know me."
"No!" Peter declared emphatically. "Even if I have to die with you, I will never deny you!" And all the others vowed the same.

(Mark 14:27–31)

WHEN JESUS INTERACTED with His disciples, no opportunity was lost. In this passage, they had just finished the Last Supper before His death. They had experienced and celebrated communion and learned that remembrance would be a vital part of their times together in the future.

Little did they understand the significance or comfort this would be in the days ahead. And yet their leader, Jesus, knew and understood— and He prepared the way for them.

During this time, He also had to speak truth. He did so factually and straightforwardly even though He knew they wouldn't yet see the whole picture. It was a weighty message: they would all desert Him, yet He would go ahead of them into Galilee. Peter was so adamant that he would never desert Jesus that he couldn't even fathom it. Neither could the other disciples and they vowed that this wouldn't happen.

I wonder how Jesus measured His emotions in the knowledge He held of these last significant moments? He knew what was best for His disciples and had to navigate the tension between His emotions and the reality.

I sense that Jesus lived out for us what Paul says in 1 Corinthians 4:2. Paul reminds us that we refuse to have anything to do with shameful deeds and underhanded ways. We don't use trickery, nor do we distort what God has told us in the Bible. We choose truth, and those around us who are honest themselves know this. This is our testimony.

As I facilitated a leadership cohort for a, intelligent and compassionate group of women who came from other countries and were fresh to their leadership roles, they brought some challenging conversations to the table to discuss.

A woman named Arianna shared that she had a challenging conversation coming up that was creating a lot of stress for her. It was stressful, as she had to handle a difficult situation with one of her employees and it was messy; on top of that, she would be leaving her job soon to move to another city. The easy way out would have been to leave this particular conversation for the person who had to take over her responsibilities.

Instead, the strength and support of her team gave her the courage and wisdom to leave well by finishing what was hers to finish. Her team assured her that she wasn't alone as she addressed this situation. They assured her that they would have her back immediately after the conversation and once she had moved on. Her work would not be momentary; it would have a lasting effect in and through her teammates.

KALEIDOSCOPE REFLECTIONS

1. As a leader, what is your greatest fear when a difficult conversation is needed?

2. Think of a recent difficult conversation that you skirted. How would you describe the value of yours that stopped you from having the conversation? How could this affect your leadership influence?

3. What is your greatest need in having a difficult conversation? Is it skills, courage, focus, planned outcome, or addressing your fear of the repercussions?

4. How would you describe your ability to have lifegiving conversations that flow with grace and truth even when goodbyes complicate the situation?

5. What can you glean from the above passage that you may not have seen before about Jesus and His leadership and how He chose to say goodbye?

6. What is one step you can take in moving forward and being more courageous and lifegiving in the area of difficult conversations?

CHAPTER TWENTY-FIVE
WHEN CLOSE RELATIONSHIPS DISAPPOINT

They went to the olive grove called Gethsemane, and Jesus said, "Sit here while I go and pray." He took Peter, James, and John with him, and he became deeply troubled and distressed. He told them, "My soul is crushed with grief to the point of death. Stay here and keep watch with me."

He went on a little farther and fell to the ground. He prayed that, if it were possible, the awful hour awaiting him might pass him by. "Abba, Father," he cried out, "everything is possible for you. Please take this cup of suffering away from me. Yet I want your will to be done, not mine."

Then he returned and found the disciples asleep. He said to Peter, "Simon, are you asleep? Couldn't you watch with me even one hour? Keep watch and pray, so that you will not give in to temptation. For the spirit is willing, but the body is weak."

Then Jesus left them again and prayed the same prayer as before. When he returned to them again, he found them sleeping, for they couldn't keep their eyes open. And they didn't know what to say.

When he returned to them the third time, he said, "Go ahead and sleep. Have your rest. But no—the time has come. The Son of Man is betrayed into the hands of sinners. Up, let's be going. Look, my betrayer is here!"

(Mark 14:32–42)

THIS WOULD BE a heartbreaking scene of abandoned friendship for anyone. Walk with me through the olive grove in the Garden of Gethsemane at twilight holds an air of heaviness as the faint rays of sunlight filter through the trees, creating deep shadows.

Walking through these shadowed olive trees, Jesus's mind is heavy for the future as grief tears at His heart. From this heart overwhelmed by grief, words pour out of His mouth to the disciples: "As you sit here, pray that temptation does not overcome you."

Walking away, He falls to His knees and pleads with His Father to take away the cup of suffering ahead, but He wants to accomplish His Father's will, not His own.

In that sacred moment of submission, as an angel appears to strengthen Him, His prayers became even more fervent. Sweat rolls down His forehead onto the ground like great drops of blood.

Slowly, ever so slowly, He rises from His knees and goes out to find His friends, the disciples. But exhausted from their grief, they have fallen asleep.

Weary, worn from grief, and grappling with submission to His Father's will, these passionate words are torn from His lips: "Why are you sleeping? Come on, get up, pray. If you don't, you will be overpowered by temptation."

Jesus then returns to His disciples to find the very man, Peter, who said he would never desert His Lord; he is fast asleep, totally unaware of the agony of heart and soul His Lord is facing.

Picture the disappointment Jesus experienced in these friends. His situation was overwhelming and once again Jesus poured out prayers to His Abba Father. Three times this same scene unfolded as Jesus faced His moment of greatest betrayal.

The third time He found His disciples asleep, He let them know that it was time to be up and to get going together even though He knew the moment of His betrayal was at hand.

I haven't faced such a painful betrayal as this one, yet I have had my own experiences and walked with others who have almost drowned in the pain of loss. I've watched the pain radiate from their eyes, bodies, and hearts. I've seen the disappointment, disillusionment, frustration, and anger. I've sat with the pain of the unfairness of life and even anger towards God. I've sat where there were no answers, no fixes, and no revelations—simply lives that are changed forever.

In this moment of writing, I feel the hopelessness and sense of defeat. Yet I also know the One who has conquered the power of sin, betrayal, and death. I know He is able. He is able because He has provided a way to live beyond our pain and hurt.

In this story, Jesus shows us the depth of His relationship with His Father, the perseverance that is required. He demonstrates the inner knowledge that allows Him to navigate these last hours with those He loved in spite of their lack of presence with Him in His hour of need. Jesus again delivered hope in the midst of hopelessness.

KALEIDOSCOPE REFLECTIONS

1. Have you experienced a soul crushed with grief, the grief of what lies ahead, of the fickleness of friends at the most crucial of times? Describe your most crushing leadership moment with friends.

2. How would you describe what was most devastating to you in this crushing leadership moment?

3. How far has your pain reached towards destroying what has God called and created you for?

4. How has your identity in Christ been tampered with and become a false identity?

5. In what ways has shame or blame become your coping mechanism?

6. Are you ready to start the healing journey?

7. Who is one person with whom you can walk this journey?

8. Call them....

CHAPTER TWENTY-SIX
THE ULTIMATE PRICE OF LEADERSHIP

And immediately, even as Jesus said this, Judas, one of the twelve disciples, arrived with a crowd of men armed with swords and clubs. They had been sent by the leading priests, the teachers of religious law, and the elders. The traitor, Judas, had given them a prearranged signal: "You will know which one to arrest when I greet him with a kiss. Then you can take him away under guard." As soon as they arrived, Judas walked up to Jesus. "Rabbi!" he exclaimed, and gave him the kiss.

Then the others grabbed Jesus and arrested him. But one of the men with Jesus pulled out his sword and struck the high priest's slave, slashing off his ear.

Jesus asked them, "Am I some dangerous revolutionary, that you come with swords and clubs to arrest me? Why didn't you arrest me in the Temple? I was there among you teaching every day. But these things are happening to fulfill what the Scriptures say about me."

Then all his disciples deserted him and ran away. One young man following behind was clothed only in a long linen shirt. When the mob tried to grab him, he slipped out of his shirt and ran away naked.

(Mark 14:43–52)[21]

HOW OFTEN I have read this portion of Mark with Easter eyes, focused on the story of Jesus and His betrayal, crucifixion, death, and resurrection. I've discovered the challenge of reading this passage with leadership eyes, watching Jesus as He continued to lead and be who He said He was, even in the face of death.

---

[21] Take the time to read and dwell for a few moments on Mark 15 as you approach this theme.

I invite you to pick up the challenge to read these passages with leadership eyes. Close your Easter eyes and see Jesus as your ultimate leader. Take the time to read this passage several times, letting the weight of His leadership grip your mind and soul.

As I was reading and pondering what to write, I felt that my words were all too small for the magnitude of the story. I felt God embrace me while He painted a picture of servant leadership beyond my true comprehension. I continue to ponder the truth that Jesus wasn't just a great role model; He was the ultimate servant leader.

In John 10:10, He came to give life in all its fullness.

In John 12:49, He didn't speak based on His own authority, but on the authority of His Father in heaven.

John 12:50, He knew that His Father's words led to eternal life and so He spoke those words of power.

John 13:1–20, He knew who sent Him, what He was to do, and that one day He would answer to His heavenly Father again.

John 14:1–14, He knew what lay ahead and the grandeur that filled heaven.

Jesus knew. He listened. He obeyed. He believed His Father. He lived what He knew. He prepared the way for the Holy Spirit so that we, too, could live in the confidence of our own creation and calling.

And so I leave you with the challenge to sit in these verses and let God's truth and wisdom wash over you as you seek to understand and embrace who servant leaders are and what they do.

KALEIDOSCOPE REFLECTIONS

1. As you read these verses with leadership eyes, in what ways does your perception of Jesus as our servant leader shift or perhaps become clearer? Describe that shift or sense of clarity.

2. What message does your heart receive through this time of reflection and deeper understanding?

3. Knowing your call to be a servant leader, describe what you sense God calling you to do and be in this moment.

4. Do you have someone to process this with? If so, who? And when will you do it?

PART SIX
UNDERSTANDING POWER AND AUTHORITY

> We work for peace every time we exercise authority with wisdom and authentic love.[22]
>
> —Jean Vanier

UNDERSTANDING POWER AND authority comes more clearly when you have a true realization of who sent you, what they sent you to do, and when they expect you to come home with the job done.

As a child, my mom and I often went to the little corner store. It was run by the Koo family who lived down the hill and around the corner from our house. The Koo family spoke limited English, yet their customer service was remarkable.

One day my mom wrote me a grocery list, read it through with me, gave me the cash to pay for the items, and then sent me off on my first adventure alone to the corner store. I felt so brave and trusted as I walked down that steep hill, crossing the road twice, and stepped into Koo's Corner Grocery. I was sure everyone who met me on the way saw my bravery and how trustworthy I was.

I pushed the bright red door open and confidently walked up to the counter and gave Mr. Koo my order. He pointed out where I would find everything on the list and then went over the items as he bagged them

---

[22] Jean Vanier, *Finding Peace* (Toronto, ON: House of Anansi, 2003), 42.

for me. I carefully counted out the cash and handed it to him. His eyes twinkled as he smiled knowingly at me and gave me the change.

After thanking him, I tugged that bright red door open, looked both ways, and tackled the hill again, standing a little taller knowing that I had done just what I had been asked to do. Now I could hand the groceries over to my mom having completed the task. As I approached home, I just knew that my mom would be waiting with a big smile on her face and a few questions on her lips. It was one of my first tastes of being given power that hadn't been entrusted to me before and of being held accountable to complete a task well on my own.

Long before I ever read or understood John 13, I was shown how to live it. Mom sent me on an errand, gave me a job to do, and I returned with the job completed. It was a picture of empowerment and accountability, coming to know and experience healthy power and authority.

CHAPTER TWENTY-SEVEN
TEACHING WITH AUTHORITY

Jesus and his companions went to the town of Capernaum. When the Sabbath day came, he went into the synagogue and began to teach. The people were amazed at his teaching, for he taught with real authority—quite unlike the teachers of religious law.

Suddenly, a man in the synagogue who was possessed by an evil spirit cried out, "Why are you interfering with us, Jesus of Nazareth? Have you come to destroy us? I know who you are—the Holy One of God!"

But Jesus reprimanded him. "Be quiet! Come out of the man," he ordered. At that, the evil spirit screamed, threw the man into a convulsion, and then came out of him.

Amazement gripped the audience, and they began to discuss what had happened. "What sort of new teaching is this?" they asked excitedly. "It has such authority! Even evil spirits obey his orders!" The news about Jesus spread quickly throughout the entire region of Galilee.

(Mark 1:21–28)[23]

ALTHOUGH THE TEMPLE was in Jerusalem, for many people it was too far from the smaller towns to travel to. Since the time of Ezra (450 BC), a group of ten Jewish families could start their own synagogue. This meant that synagogues could be established in other towns.

During the week, Jewish boys were taught the Old Testament Law and Jewish religion. Girls weren't allowed to attend. This explains Paul's comment in 2 Timothy 2:11–12 when He said that women aren't allowed to teach men or have authority over them.

---

[23] See also Luke 4:31–37.

One interpretation that makes sense is that women didn't teach because they weren't given the opportunity to have an education. Men were given an education and were allowed to teach. Education was one form of authority present in the teaching the men provided.

The synagogues often hosted guest teachers, and so on this occasion Jesus taught in the synagogue at Capernaum. The original text describes the people as being astonished at His teaching—astonished, meaning that His teaching struck them with intense amazement.

Jesus's teaching was filled with real and genuine authority. The difference between Christ's teaching and the teaching of the Scribes and Pharisees is that He seemed to have direct authority from God. Although steeped in history and culture, the Pharisees' teaching carried no life or conviction.

As sons and daughters of Jesus Christ, we bring a sweet aroma of the beauty, strength, power, and light only God can anoint us with. It far exceeds what we can do in our own strength, and it's one of the most humbling and exhilarating truths we have been blessed to walk in.

KALEIDOSCOPE REFLECTIONS

1. What qualifies a person to teach?

2. Could an ordinary person teach with the same strength as Jesus? If so, what would cause that kind of teaching to happen? If not, why not?

3. Do you ever serve in the role of teacher? What do you see as your responsibilities as a teacher?

4. What would make you the kind of teacher we see modelled in Jesus's life?

5. As a student, what responsibilities do you have? How would you behave as a student if Jesus was your teacher?

CHAPTER TWENTY-EIGHT
BRAVE DEPENDENCE ON GOD LACED WITH HUMBLE AUTHORITY

After Jesus crossed over by boat, a large crowd met him at the seaside. One of the meeting-place leaders named Jairus came. When he saw Jesus, he fell to his knees, beside himself as he begged, "My dear daughter is at death's door. Come and lay hands on her so she will get well and live." Jesus went with him, the whole crowd tagging along, pushing and jostling him.

A woman who had suffered a condition of hemorrhaging for twelve years—a long succession of physicians had treated her, and treated her badly, taking all her money and leaving her worse off than before—had heard about Jesus. She slipped in from behind and touched his robe. She was thinking to herself, "If I can put a finger on his robe, I can get well." The moment she did it, the flow of blood dried up. She could feel the change and knew her plague was over and done with.

At the same moment, Jesus felt energy discharging from him. He turned around to the crowd and asked, "Who touched my robe?"

His disciples said, "What are you talking about? With this crowd pushing and jostling you, you're asking, 'Who touched me?' Dozens have touched you!"

But he went on asking, looking around to see who had done it. The woman, knowing what had happened, knowing she was the one, stepped up in fear and trembling, knelt before him, and gave him the whole story.

Jesus said to her, "Daughter, you took a risk of faith, and now you're healed and whole. Live well, live blessed! Be healed of your plague."

While he was still talking, some people came from the leader's house and told him, "Your daughter is dead. Why bother the Teacher any more?"

Jesus overheard what they were talking about and said to the leader, "Don't listen to them; just trust me."

> *He permitted no one to go in with him except Peter, James, and John. They entered the leader's house and pushed their way through the gossips looking for a story and neighbors bringing in casseroles. Jesus was abrupt: "Why all this busybody grief and gossip? This child isn't dead; she's sleeping." Provoked to sarcasm, they told him he didn't know what he was talking about.*
>
> *But when he had sent them all out, he took the child's father and mother, along with his companions, and entered the child's room. He clasped the girl's hand and said, "Talitha koum," which means, "Little girl, get up." At that, she was up and walking around! This girl was twelve years of age. They, of course, were all beside themselves with joy. He gave them strict orders that no one was to know what had taken place in that room. Then he said, "Give her something to eat."*
>
> (Mark 5:21–43, MSG)

I LOVE THE picture of Jesus we see in this passage. It's such an emotional time of stress, grief, and suffering for Jairus and his family, as well as for the woman with the issue of bleeding.

It was already a dramatic day, with a heart-stopping storm, demon-possessed pigs set free, and then Jesus stepping into a boat to escape the crowds. And now a heartbroken father falls on his knees before Jesus, desperately pleading for his daughter's life.

Right on the heels of all of this emotional and heart-rending work, a woman, desperate for healing and health, someone who had nothing to lose and everything to gain, came surreptitiously up behind Jesus and touched the hem of His garment, drawing His healing power from Him—and He knew it.

In both these stories, the crowds were close around Jesus. He had the ideal opportunity to grandstand and bring attention to Himself. Instead He chose to pay attention to those around Him—to sense their need, pain, and suffering. He chose to respond with compassion, grace, and a call for them to obey what He asked them to do.

He moved with purpose in spite of His disciples questioning Him and the crowds laughing at Him. He was so in tune with His Father's heart and purpose for Him that He calmly and assuredly did that which was true to who He had been called to be. He saw the person, felt their need, met them where they were at, and healed them.

KALEIDOSCOPE REFLECTIONS

1. In the midst of the daily pressures, when was the last time you really saw and sensed the needs of those around you? Describe what you saw and felt in those moments.

2. Even if your first response isn't the same as what you see in Jesus in these stories, do you grasp that He is with you? Do you believe He will give you wisdom for what is yours and what isn't? Describe what it looks like when you recognize that you're out of energy and don't have the patience you think you could have.

3. Stop and reflect on what it would look like to have brave dependence on God when you're stressed and stretched. If you can see it, you can move towards it.

4. Stop and reflect on what it would look like to walk in humble authority. Ask God for the grace and courage to live in that space when you feel you have nothing else to give.

5. As a result of these reflections, in what ways might you be taking on more than is yours? Where do you need to realign or shift your thinking, attitudes, and behaviours?

CHAPTER TWENTY-NINE
UNBELIEF KILLS POWER

Jesus left that part of the country and returned with his disciples to Nazareth, his hometown. The next Sabbath he began teaching in the synagogue, and many who heard him were amazed. They asked, "Where did he get all this wisdom and the power to perform such miracles?" Then they scoffed, "He's just a carpenter, the son of Mary and the brother of James, Joseph, Judas, and Simon. And his sisters live right here among us." They were deeply offended and refused to believe in him.

Then Jesus told them, "A prophet is honored everywhere except in his own hometown and among his relatives and his own family." And because of their unbelief, he couldn't do any miracles among them except to place his hands on a few sick people and heal them. And he was amazed at their unbelief.

(Mark 6:1–6)

YOU MIGHT EXPECT to experience the greatest acceptance when you return to your hometown later in life, bringing with you your gifts and talents. Then why is it that your hometown is often the toughest place to return to? It's not uncommon to be faced with rejection and even mockery when one returns home. Too often we are diminished by the ones who at one time knew us well.

The fear of being an imposter haunted me when I was asked to go back to the area where I grew up and be the keynote speaker at a leadership conference. With this invitation, I was no longer returning as my parents' daughter; I was returning because some people believed I had something to offer that they needed. It was nerve-wracking, yet it became a place of affirmation in my leadership journey. The reception I received was warm and authentic and our time together was rich with stories, learnings, and growth.

Perhaps because of that experience, I could relate to this story so well.

I realized as I read this story that I was in good company as the people of Jesus's hometown of Nazareth watched Him return. They were overcome with amazement at His preaching, wondering where He had gotten this wisdom and the power to perform miracles.

And yet within moments they became deeply offended and refused to believe in Him. What an emotional rollercoaster! This switch of outlook served to limit what Jesus could do for them. Only a few of His touches resulted in healing, and that was all. Even Jesus was amazed at the extent of their unbelief.

Interestingly, this became a turning point for Jesus to send His disciples out two by two. It was time for them to spread their wings. He had called them, built relationship with them, trained them, and modelled ministry to them. He'd watched them minister and now they were to go out in pairs continue on without Him.

Jesus had set them up to walk in His ways and to handle life as it came because of their front seat view to His incredible earthly journey.

KALEIDOSCOPE REFLECTIONS

1. Have you had the experience of returning to your hometown, or even to your old ministry, for a visit? Describe what it was like. Were there any high points or low points? Any surprises?

2. That which had the potential for discouragement and defeat, Jesus turned into a far greater opportunity for multiplied ministry. In this story, we see His turning point in releasing the disciples for greater ministry on their own than they had ever known. Take the time to describe the discipling process you follow. How would you describe your discipling philosophy?

3. How has this story impacted your understanding of leadership? How are you embracing the opportunity to live out the call to see others grow in their faith and walk with God?

CHAPTER THIRTY
HEAVENLY POWER

The Pharisees, along with some religion scholars who had come from Jerusalem, gathered around him. They noticed that some of his disciples weren't being careful with ritual washings before meals. The Pharisees—Jews in general, in fact—would never eat a meal without going through the motions of a ritual hand-washing, with an especially vigorous scrubbing if they had just come from the market (to say nothing of the scourings they'd give jugs and pots and pans).

The Pharisees and religion scholars asked, "Why do your disciples brush off the rules, showing up at meals without washing their hands?"

Jesus answered, "Isaiah was right about frauds like you, hit the bull's-eye in fact:

These people make a big show of saying the right thing, but their heart isn't in it. They act like they are worshiping me, but they don't mean it. They just use me as a cover for teaching whatever suits their fancy, ditching God's command and taking up the latest fads."

He went on, "Well, good for you. You get rid of God's command so you won't be inconvenienced in following the religious fashions! Moses said, 'Respect your father and mother,' and, 'Anyone denouncing father or mother should be killed.' But you weasel out of that by saying that it's perfectly acceptable to say to father or mother, 'Gift! What I owed you I've given as a gift to God,' thus relieving yourselves of obligation to father or mother. You scratch out God's Word and scrawl a whim in its place. You do a lot of things like this."

Jesus called the crowd together again and said, "Listen now, all of you—take this to heart. It's not what you swallow that pollutes your life; it's what you vomit—that's the real pollution."

When he was back home after being with the crowd, his disciples said, "We don't get it. Put it in plain language."

> *Jesus said, "Are you being willfully stupid? Don't you see that what you swallow can't contaminate you? It doesn't enter your heart but your stomach, works its way through the intestines, and is finally flushed." (That took care of dietary quibbling; Jesus was saying that all foods are fit to eat.)*
>
> *He went on: "It's what comes out of a person that pollutes: obscenities, lusts, thefts, murders, adulteries, greed, depravity, deceptive dealings, carousing, mean looks, slander, arrogance, foolishness—all these are vomit from the heart. There is the source of your pollution."*
>
> (Mark 7:1–23, MSG)

THE TERM "HEAVENLY POWER" isn't used in this story, and yet this is a powerful picture of how we can get set in our ways, traditions, and even sins, replacing the power of God with what seems right to us. Jesus addressed the way the Pharisees took God's commands and replaced them with their own teachings. He called them out for disregarding the law in order to protect their own traditions.

We can see His frustration with the Pharisees as He went into a house to get away from them. His last words to them were a teaching and a rebuke as He pointed out that it wasn't what they were eating that defiled them but rather what they said and did. As Jesus sat with His disciples in the house, He added for their benefit that it's a person's thought life that defiles them. It was a wake-up call to pay the most careful attention to one's heart, thought life, and actions.

Read this passage several times to catch the nuances and put it all together. Read it not so much for the truths we need to grasp as leaders, but for how Jesus chooses His actions as a leader. It presents a powerful picture of a leader who knew who had sent Him, what His purpose was, and who He was returning to. He knew there was a need to focus on what was most important. He spoke with the crowd, and His disciples, and made His message understandable. He gave voice to the condition of our hearts and the importance of our thought life being the essence of our ministry.

Time and again, we experience how simply and powerfully our thoughts can overwhelm us and take us in the wrong direction. I have been amazed at what I call the Ds of the devil: discouragement, destruction, diminishment, depression, distraction, disillusionment, distrust, despair, doubt, deceit, and defeat.

The antidote is to intentionally pursue the fruit of the Spirit: love, joy, peace, goodness, kindness, gentleness, faithfulness, self-control, and patience. We must learn to focus on becoming more loving, kind, gentle, faithful, joyful, peaceful, patient, self-controlled, and filled with goodness.

Heavenly power is evidenced in a heart that chooses to lean into the purposes of God, to walk in obedience to the winds of the Holy Spirit. As we pay attention, we find our hearts captured by a call that is much bigger than our own thoughts and plans. We find ourselves expanding and overflowing with the fruit of God's Holy Spirit.

KALEIDOSCOPE REFLECTIONS

1. After reading this passage several times to be aware of how Jesus chose His actions, take some quiet time to reflect on how He led.

2. Reflect on Jesus's leadership and what gave Him the strength to act the way He did.

3. What has become clear to you through Jesus's example and any potential areas for your growth?

4. Reflect on where you spend the most effort: is it your actions, your heart, or your thoughts? In considering Jesus's words and actions, describe where you see the need to shift how you address these issues.

5. What is one thing you will put into practice because of the way the Holy Spirit spoke to you from this passage?

CHAPTER THIRTY-ONE
THE TENSION BETWEEN THE POWER OF JESUS'S NAME AND THE POWER OF SIN

John said to Jesus, "Teacher, we saw someone using your name to cast out demons, but we told him to stop because he wasn't in our group."
"Don't stop him!" Jesus said. "No one who performs a miracle in my name will soon be able to speak evil of me. Anyone who is not against us is for us. If anyone gives you even a cup of water because you belong to the Messiah, I tell you the truth, that person will surely be rewarded.
"But if you cause one of these little ones who trusts in me to fall into sin, it would be better for you to be thrown into the sea with a large millstone hung around your neck. If your hand causes you to sin, cut it off. It's better to enter eternal life with only one hand than to go into the unquenchable fires of hell with two hands. If your foot causes you to sin, cut it off. It's better to enter eternal life with only one foot than to be thrown into hell with two feet. And if your eye causes you to sin, gouge it out. It's better to enter the Kingdom of God with only one eye than to have two eyes and be thrown into hell, 'where the maggots never die and the fire never goes out.'
"For everyone will be tested with fire. Salt is good for seasoning. But if it loses its flavor, how do you make it salty again? You must have the qualities of salt among yourselves and live in peace with each other."
(Mark 9:38–50)

AFTER A CHASTISING conversation with His disciples on the topic of greatness, John tells Jesus about what they just did. I think John was considering the disciples' actions to be honourable and good. They had watched someone outside their group cast out demons in Jesus's name. But because he hadn't been part of their group, they'd told him to stop.

Jesus's reaction was quick and sure, since He understood the power of someone using His name. If they used His name to perform miracles, before long people wouldn't be able to speak evil of Jesus at all. He was clear with the disciples that if anyone gave them a cup of water in the Messiah's name, the water giver would be rewarded.

This was like a twist of the kaleidoscope. The disciples so wanted to please their Lord and honour Him. To them, it seemed simple that people who weren't in a relationship with Jesus shouldn't be able to speak in His name. This seemed wrong, yet the power of the name of Jesus is greater than the power of sin.

The disciples who had the privilege of walking and talking with Jesus in person didn't yet know what Paul taught us in Philippians 2:5–11. The challenge is to embrace the attitude that Jesus embraced and with which He served His Father and others—an attitude that would lead Him to a criminal's death yet provide grace and life for those who choose to believe. This attitude will eventually lead to every knee bowing before Him and every tongue confessing that He is Lord. It's a beautiful passage to dwell on and it can allow us to shift our way of thinking.

Jesus wasn't into exclusion. He was into inclusion and invitation into His life and world. He didn't stop those who spoke His name, whether they knew Him personally or not. And His challenge to those He influenced was to deal with sin before it destroys you.

Jesus uses salt as the last metaphor in this passage. Salt has many appealing properties:

- It changes hard water to soft water.
- It cleanses and helps clear up infections.
- It acts as a preservative for vegetables as pickles, meats, and seafood.
- It melts ice.
- It creates thirst.
- It heals canker sources when used as a mouth wash.
- It soothes sore throats when gargled with water.
- It makes food more flavourful.

These are just a few of the uses of salt. Jesus admonished us to have the qualities of salt in order to live at peace with each other.

Focus on being salt… salt that preserves rather than destroys, and that adds flavour rather than being bland. Salt creates a healthy environment.

Oh, the privilege of having a leader who knew how to empower and hold His followers accountable! Jesus knew how to speak in metaphors His followers could relate to, learn from, and grow by.

KALEIDOSCOPE REFLECTIONS

1. This is a heart-searching question. Have you ever spoken poorly of someone who isn't in your group? Have you ever spoken poorly of someone in another denomination or church because you feel your beliefs are right and theirs are wrong?

2. As you reread this passage, are you courageous enough to let go of the power of sin in your life and cling to the power of Jesus's name by learning to live out the qualities of salt?

3. What would it look like in your life to be more salty in your faith, and why would you consider this important in light of your call and purpose?

CHAPTER THIRTY-TWO
KEEP WATCH AND PRAY

As he walked away from the Temple, one of his disciples said, *"Teacher, look at that stonework! Those buildings!"*

Jesus said, *"You're impressed by this grandiose architecture? There's not a stone in the whole works that is not going to end up in a heap of rubble."*

Later, as he was sitting on Mount Olives in full view of the Temple, Peter, James, John, and Andrew got him off by himself and asked, *"Tell us, when is this going to happen? What sign will we get that things are coming to a head?"*

Jesus began, *"Watch out for doomsday deceivers. Many leaders are going to show up with forged identities claiming, 'I'm the One.' They will deceive a lot of people. When you hear of wars and rumored wars, keep your head and don't panic. This is routine history, and no sign of the end. Nation will fight nation and ruler fight ruler, over and over. Earthquakes will occur in various places. There will be famines. But these things are nothing compared to what's coming.*

"And watch out! They're going to drag you into court. And then it will go from bad to worse, dog-eat-dog, everyone at your throat because you carry my name. You're placed there as sentinels to truth. The Message has to be preached all across the world.

"When they bring you, betrayed, into court, don't worry about what you'll say. When the time comes, say what's on your heart—the Holy Spirit will make his witness in and through you.

"It's going to be brother killing brother, father killing child, children killing parents. There's no telling who will hate you because of me.

"Stay with it—that's what is required. Stay with it to the end. You won't be sorry; you'll be saved.

"But be ready to run for it when you see the monster of desecration set up where it should never be. You who can read, make sure you understand what

> I'm talking about. If you're living in Judea at the time, run for the hills; if you're working in the yard, don't go back to the house to get anything; if you're out in the field, don't go back to get your coat. Pregnant and nursing mothers will have it especially hard. Hope and pray this won't happen in the middle of winter.
>
> "These are going to be hard days—nothing like it from the time God made the world right up to the present. And there'll be nothing like it again. If he let the days of trouble run their course, nobody would make it. But because of God's chosen people, those he personally chose, he has already intervened.
>
> "If anyone tries to flag you down, calling out, 'Here's the Messiah!' or points, 'There he is!' don't fall for it. Fake Messiahs and lying preachers are going to pop up everywhere. Their impressive credentials and bewitching performances will pull the wool over the eyes of even those who ought to know better. So watch out. I've given you fair warning.
>
> "Following those hard times, Sun will fade out, moon cloud over, stars fall out of the sky, cosmic powers tremble.
>
> "And then they'll see the Son of Man enter in grand style, his Arrival filling the sky—no one will miss it! He'll dispatch the angels; they will pull in the chosen from the four winds, from pole to pole.
>
> "Take a lesson from the fig tree. From the moment you notice its buds form, the merest hint of green, you know summer's just around the corner. And so it is with you. When you see all these things, you know he is at the door. Don't take this lightly. I'm not just saying this for some future generation, but for this one, too—these things will happen. Sky and earth will wear out; my words won't wear out.
>
> "But the exact day and hour? No one knows that, not even heaven's angels, not even the Son. Only the Father. So keep a sharp lookout, for you don't know the timetable. It's like a man who takes a trip, leaving home and putting his servants in charge, each assigned a task, and commanding the gatekeeper to stand watch. So, stay at your post, watching. You have no idea when the homeowner is returning, whether evening, midnight, cockcrow, or morning. You don't want him showing up unannounced, with you asleep on the job. I say it to you, and I'm saying it to all: Stay at your post. Keep watch."
>
> (Mark 13:1–37, MSG)

WHAT A POWERFUL and at times disconcerting chapter to read. There is doom and gloom here. Picture the disciples leaving the temple, a place of safety and security. Their minds are at rest, filled with a fresh sense of gratitude and appreciation for what they see in front of them. Even the architecture takes on a fresh appearance as they exclaim about the magnificence of the buildings.

Then, like a glass of cold water thrown in their faces, Jesus takes the conversation and turns it to one of daunting prophecy.

Jesus's words about the future served to create a kind of knowledge that enabled the disciples to live more fully in the present with an eye to the future. He painted clarity about the future, yet the timing of those events wasn't clear.

For us today, the timing of our future is no more clear than it was for the disciples. And so we live in the present, aware of a coming future that invites and compels us to remain faithful to God's call on our hearts and lives.

At many times in history, the church has faced challenging situations that gave rise to opportunities to consider about the church is of utmost importance. We often pray and ask God to show us what lies ahead.

In this chapter, He does just that with His disciples. We don't have the privilege of seeing their reaction to all this news. At the beginning of the conversation they were intrigued, which we know by Jesus's response to their admiration of the buildings. They asked for more information and received far more than they were prepared for.

There are times in leadership when your people won't fully understand where you're coming from as you prepare them for a new future which holds discomfort and will require them to let go and embrace something different.

In this story, we see that Jesus revealed the most details and clarity to the people He had the closest relationships with. This is a principle in casting vision. The people we're closest to in leadership are given the most information, as they'll play a part in paving the way forward and seeing the vision to fruition

So, as we consider this passage, the point isn't the content as much as it is seeing how Jesus as their leader delivered this difficult foreshadowing. It's about what we observe about His presence with the disciples.

KALEIDOSCOPE REFLECTIONS

1. Identify what you feel as you finish reading this passage. Reflect on how you manage your different feelings as you lead and influence others through a difficult time.

2. Reflect on how you gain strength and what you do to focus on what's of most importance when your emotions are deeply stirred and when you have to help others through emotionally charged situations.

3. Based on how you use emotion and fact together in challenging times, how could you better help others think through their reactions or responses?

4. How can you continue to develop your circle of influence by entrusting the vision you carry to others?

PART SEVEN
EMPOWERING OTHERS

> The heart of empowerment lies in the ability to see people where they are at and to inspire them to dream, to learn and, to grow to their full potential.
> —Ruth Esau

I LOVE THE words empower, entrust, invest, and equip. They open the door for using diversity to create unity as we learn to live and work together, our unique qualities help to achieve a greater purpose than what we could achieve on our own. I consider it a privilege to watch others accomplish and thrive in ways I never could. When we all bring our best to the table, the end product is better.

Focusing on how we choose to see people, knowing and hearing them, will draw the best from them. At times this means seeing what they don't see, and at other times it means providing training in areas of technical or professional development to imbue them with a greater level of confidence and competence.

In 2007, I was privileged to be invited into a partnership with Corey Olynik, the co-founder of Executive Directions with Wayne Stewart. A key promise of ExD, which facilitated leadership development with executive leaders, was that those who participated fully would increase their competence and confidence. Over time our promise was realized again and again in the lives of incredible leaders.

The twist is that as we started out, we believed that if we gave people more skills and increased their competence, their confidence would naturally increase. It didn't work out that way. Instead their confidence grew as they honoured each other. With the wisdom each one brought to the table, they learned to give and take in fresh ways that created space for trust and growth.

We were privileged to create, participate in, and invite others into a leadership development culture that empowered them and increased their circles of influence.

Often people of faith would say to me, "You know that what you're doing is discipleship, right?" And yes, I did know that. The greatest example of empowering people came from the life of Jesus Christ, who is my dearest friend.

Come and consider Jesus's example to us.

CHAPTER THIRTY-THREE
AS HE WAS WALKING

Later on, after John was arrested, Jesus went into Galilee, where he preached God's Good News. "The time promised by God has come at last!" he announced. "The Kingdom of God is near! Repent of your sins and believe the Good News!"

One day as Jesus was walking along the shore of the Sea of Galilee, he saw Simon and his brother Andrew throwing a net into the water, for they fished for a living. Jesus called out to them, "Come, follow me, and I will show you how to fish for people!" And they left their nets at once and followed him.

A little farther up the shore Jesus saw Zebedee's sons, James and John, in a boat repairing their nets. He called them at once, and they also followed him, leaving their father, Zebedee, in the boat with the hired men.

(Mark 1:14–20)[24]

THIS PASSAGE COMES on the heels of John's announcement of Jesus's arrival, His baptism (when He received the approval of God His Father), His temptation for forty days in the wilderness, and John's arrest. We hear and sense Jesus's words, perhaps of frustration and also of anticipation: "At last the time has come! The Kingdom of God is near! Turn from your sins and believe this Good News!"

Jesus's ministry had begun and now was the time for Him to find and call those who would walk with Him. This is the background to the walk Jesus took along the shore of Galilee, where He reached out to ask a few chosen ones: "Come, be My disciples, and I'll show you how to fish for people."

---

[24] See also Matthew 4:18–22 and Luke 5: 1–11.

Jesus's twofold invitation was to Himself, as if He were saying, "First come hang out with Me. Get close to Me. Trust Me, Emulate Me. Love Me. Then I will show you how to attract people for the sake of the Kingdom."

His earthly ministry had just begun. He knew what He had to do, so He began to find the people to make it happen. He looked for those to whom He would entrust His life changing message to.

Even here, we may question how He chose the ones who were to be closest to Him. Simply put, He paid attention to those around Him as He walked. He watched until He saw what He was looking for and then He invited them into His world, while He met them in their worlds.

Walking is a great analogy for the lifestyle of discipleship. So often we limit discipleship to our efforts to get others to accept Jesus and participate in the programs we provide for their benefit. If we have a personal relationship with Jesus Christ, discipleship can be so much more. It's the journey of life we are privileged to walk together.

In the late 1990s, as I was privileged to walk with others as a pastor, my heart became burdened to be more intentional with a number of women who had asked to spend time with me. Many had asked me to mentor them. I chose not to say yes right off the bat, but I did commit to praying for them.

As the list of names grew, however, I sensed God saying, "Invite them to a group." For some time I argued back with God that mentoring didn't happen in a group; it was one to one. But God persisted in bringing this group mentoring idea to my attention—until I finally said, "I'll go to the bookstore and get a book that tells me how to do this."

To the delight of my resistant heart, there was no book. And God didn't let this go.

Finally, I gave in.

"Fine," I said. "But you're going to have to tell me what to do and who to invite."

And of course, true to form, God did just that. As I waited on His Holy Spirit, I received the wisdom and grace to move forward and start what I later came to call Women of Influence, or WOI. And here we are in 2021, still going strong. God continues to call, guide, and challenge and comfort us as we navigate life together. Many of these women have reached out to other women in their circles of influence and poured their own lives into them. Together we have walked through joys, sorrows, disappointments, celebrations, changes, sickness, healing, death, and everything in between. What a joy it is to walk and figure life out together!

Walking with someone speaks to intentionality—the intentionality of knowing how to pay attention to yourself and the one you're walking with. Paying attention to the places you walk, the conversation you participate in, the sense of belonging and purpose. It's a choice to journey together and it will change your life and the lives of those you walk with.

Jesus walked with His disciples as He leaned into His Father's purposes with and through them.

KALEIDOSCOPE REFLECTIONS

1. Look at Jesus's twofold invitation. What do you glean from the way this invitation is given?

2. When you think of accomplishing ministry, do you tend to think about what you have to do? Or do you think about the people you'll need in your life for that ministry to happen? What thoughts are stirring within you?

3. Do we just look for believers or do we look for people who need to be fished from their life of sin, find peace with God, and come to know His call upon their lives?

4. Who are you seeing as you walk? Prayerfully consider why you might be seeing them and what could you do.

CHAPTER THIRTY-FOUR
CHOOSING YOUR LEADERS

> *Afterward Jesus went up on a mountain and called out the ones he wanted to go with him. And they came to him. Then he appointed twelve of them and called them his apostles. They were to accompany him, and he would send them out to preach, giving them authority to cast out demons. These are the twelve he chose: Simon (whom he named Peter), James and John (the sons of Zebedee, but Jesus nicknamed them "Sons of Thunder"), Andrew, Philip, Bartholomew, Matthew, Thomas, James (son of Alphaeus), Thaddaeus, Simon (the zealot), Judas Iscariot (who later betrayed him).*
>
> (Mark 3:13–19)[25]

SOON AFTER THIS, Jesus spent all night talking to His Father. The next morning, as the sun rose, He chose twelve of His disciples to be apostles. He sent them out to live the life He'd lived with them, sharing it with others. He sent them out to preach, teach, and heal the sick, even giving them the authority to cast out demons.

A disciple is a follower of someone, or a person trained by another. An apostle, on the other hand, is someone who's sent to carry a message. These terms are often used interchangeably in the New Testament. In the Gospels, Jesus gives His Great Commission to the disciples. In the book of Acts, they are referred to as apostles.

Mark paints a beautiful picture of diversity as he describes the ones Jesus called to follow Him. They were not ready-made leaders. They

---
[25] See also Luke 6:12–16.

were not all deeply respected. They did not display unusual or well-developed talents. What set them apart and qualified them was that in that moment of being called they were willing to obey Him.

As we know in hindsight, they didn't all stay true to that first obedience to Jesus. And yet Jesus chose them, invested in them, and entrusted His work to them by empowering them by His life and offering them a trusted relationship with Him.

One of the greatest joys of leadership comes from knowing what most needs to be passed on, and knowing who to invite into that journey with you. The joy that follows is to see how great others in their unique creation can turn out to be when they accept an assignment, being invested in and empowered for service.

Over the years, I've been privileged to have been mentored by both men and women of God, who saw in me what I didn't see in myself until they stepped into my life and created a safe space for me to be challenged, questioned, embrace fresh learnings, and grow.

Evelyn, to whom this book is dedicated, was one of those precious Jesus lovers and joy givers who took me under her wing. She started as my Old Testament professor in my Bible college days. A few years after Bible college, we began meeting for coffee or lunch occasionally, which led to us getting together regularly for years until she was no longer able to.

Evelyn knew how to rejoice and weep with me. She knew how to inspire me, affirm me, and challenge me. I anticipated our times together. We served at camp together, too. She started out as the teacher and I will never forget the day I was asked to take her place. A part of me didn't want to do it because I didn't think I could ever fill her shoes. Evelyn was the one who challenged me to "see" that when I didn't think I was good enough, I was saying no to God and figuratively telling Him that He didn't know what He was doing. I learned to repent of those thoughts and give God my yes.

Shortly before her homegoing, as I was thanking Evelyn for who she was to me and for taking so much time to be with me and journey with me, she told me about the first time she met me.

"You were the first one to come sauntering into the classroom and simply drape yourself into a desk," she said. "You reminded me of a long drink of water. I sensed God saying to me, 'Evelyn, she is one of my special treasures. Pay attention to her.'"

Those words, so many years later, touched my heart, brought tears to my eyes, and made me realize once again the wonder and power we have as we are called to walk together through life.

I pray that you, too, feel thirsty to journey with others in the give and take of life and find the joy of time well invested and multiplied.

KALEIDOSCOPE REFLECTIONS

1. What did Jesus do first before He chose His disciples? Describe what this means or how it could be applied to your situation as you choose leaders.

2. What was the most important qualification to be a disciple or apostle of Jesus?

3. What were your most important qualifications when you came into the leadership position you currently hold?

4. What is the difference you see between a leader and a spiritual leader?

5. What conclusions can you draw from this example in scripture?

6. What do you look for in leaders?

7. Describe the kind of person you find easiest to lead. Would that description fit you as well? Why, or why not?

8. There's an expression that say, "To be a great leader, you must be a great follower." Discuss what that means to you.

CHAPTER THIRTY-FIVE
HOW DO YOU LISTEN

Then Jesus asked them, "Would anyone light a lamp and then put it under a basket or under a bed? Of course not! A lamp is placed on a stand, where its light will shine. For everything that is hidden will eventually be brought into the open, and every secret will be brought to light. Anyone with ears to hear should listen and understand."

Then he added, "Pay close attention to what you hear. The closer you listen, the more understanding you will be given—and you will receive even more. To those who listen to my teaching, more understanding will be given. But for those who are not listening, even what little understanding they have will be taken away from them."

(Mark 4:21–25)

OUR FIRST CHALLENGE is to stop and consider the power of light to reveal even that which is the most hidden. This is a lesson in itself. None of us should think we can hide anything. Hidden thoughts, attitudes and behaviours can all be revealed by the light.

As leaders, we are taught to communicate by teaching, preaching, answering questions, and giving instructions. Rarely are we taught the flip side of communication: listening and really hearing what is being said. Often our greatest fear is that we won't know what to say in a situation.

Well, maybe that's the greatest space to be in. We really have to listen for understanding, and that may involve asking questions for clarification, revealing that we don't know it all. The beauty of the flip side of communication is that as we listen and ask, we invite people into a real conversation, and into relationship. We model for them that we both need to make this work. We affirm their worth in the contribution they make to the conversation.

What does it mean to listen? There are different nuances.

Level 1: I listen so I can talk. For example, you begin to talk about the changes our supervisor presented in the last staff meeting. As you talk, I pay attention to what you say. This brings my own experiences to mind and I prepare to speak whether you're finished or not. I'm running through all the similar stories in my brain files, and as a result I only hear a portion of what you say.

Level 2: I listen to have the information to respond. For example, you begin to talk about the changes our supervisor presented. Aspects of what we were told don't fully make sense to me. As you talk, I wait for that crucial information, and as soon as I hear it I cut you off since I've gotten what I need.

Level 3: I listen with all my senses and then ask questions for clarity. For example, you begin to talk about the changes our supervisor presented. Aspects of what we were told don't fully make sense to me. As I listen, I take the time to note your intonation and facial expressions. I also note your body language, how the location where we're standing affects your comfort level. I pay attention to the words you use.

With all this information, I allow myself to enter the space you're in before I talk. I begin to ask questions so I can understand more clearly where you're coming from.

KALEIDOSCOPE REFLECTIONS

1. Developing our listening skills is a part of developing greater emotional intelligence—which involves becoming aware of how we respond to what we hear and how our words affect each other. Discuss some techniques or skills you could develop in order to experience the conversation on a more relational level.

2. Consider the three levels of listening and how you have experienced them. How might you become more conscious of your role to listen in the conversations you take part in?

3. Describe what you're going to do to develop your listening skills. When will you start?

CHAPTER THIRTY-SIX
INSTRUCTIONS FOR THE JOURNEY

> *Then Jesus went from village to village, teaching the people. And he called his twelve disciples together and began sending them out two by two, giving them authority to cast out evil spirits. He told them to take nothing for their journey except a walking stick—no food, no traveler's bag, no money. He allowed them to wear sandals but not to take a change of clothes.*
>
> *"Wherever you go," he said, "stay in the same house until you leave town. But if any place refuses to welcome you or listen to you, shake its dust from your feet as you leave to show that you have abandoned those people to their fate."*
>
> *So the disciples went out, telling everyone they met to repent of their sins and turn to God. And they cast out many demons and healed many sick people, anointing them with olive oil.*
>
> (Mark 6:6–13)

THE TWELVE DISCIPLES have been with Jesus for some time now. They've sat at His feet. They've watched Him in many situations where He exercised His leadership with the authority He was given by His Father with humble, straightforward humility. They've eaten and travelled with Him.

Now He shifts the responsibility of sharing the good news to them. Kingdom work is now being entrusted to the disciples.

Whether you agree with what He asked them to do or not, this passage provides a glimpse at how He prepared them to go and fulfill their calling. It is principle-based with examples of methods so they could better understand what it meant in their context.

- Jesus *sent* them to go in pairs.
- Jesus *empowered* them with the skills they needed for what they were to be doing.
- Jesus *instructed* them on what they would need to take (they shouldn't take any extra baggage or focus on what wasn't necessary).
- Jesus *prepared* them for what they needed to do for their wellbeing.
- Jesus *prepared* and *empowered* them for the worst-case scenario so they would know how to handle it should it happen.

Jesus chose to work through the joys, sorrows, simplicity and complexity of the disciples' lives. He paid attention to the wisdom and guidance of His Father through the voice of the Holy Spirit.

He called them to greatness based on who they had been created to be and what they had been created to do. He called them to live their full potential and pour their lives into others. Calling them to greatness was a reminder of their creation in light of God's Kingdom purposes.

This way of being as a leader is the pattern Jesus left for us to follow. Walking with people to become all they were created to be is our most rewarding function as leaders.

KALEIDOSCOPE REFLECTIONS

1. Using the eyes of those you influence and lead, think about the mission and/or vision you are responsible for overseeing and accomplishing. Use the concepts in the principle-based template below to think through your situation. Include:
   - the necessary background information your people will need.
   - the desired outcome of their actions.
   - the skills or tools they will need.
   - preparations to show them how to handle what they face wherever they need to go.
   - instructions for how to determine what is theirs to accomplish and when to know to move on.

2. God has called you to greatness for the sake of His Kingdom. How would you describe what it would look like for you to serve in greatness?

CHAPTER THIRTY-SEVEN
CHOOSE TO EMPOWER YOUR FOLLOWERS

The apostles returned to Jesus from their ministry tour and told him all they had done and taught. Then Jesus said, "Let's go off by ourselves to a quiet place and rest awhile." He said this because there were so many people coming and going that Jesus and his apostles didn't even have time to eat.

So they left by boat for a quiet place, where they could be alone. But many people recognized them and saw them leaving, and people from many towns ran ahead along the shore and got there ahead of them. Jesus saw the huge crowd as he stepped from the boat, and he had compassion on them because they were like sheep without a shepherd. So he began teaching them many things.

(Mark 6:30–34)

About this time another large crowd had gathered, and the people ran out of food again. Jesus called his disciples and told them, "I feel sorry for these people. They have been here with me for three days, and they have nothing left to eat. If I send them home hungry, they will faint along the way. For some of them have come a long distance."

His disciples replied, "How are we supposed to find enough food to feed them out here in the wilderness?"

Jesus asked, "How much bread do you have?"

"Seven loaves," they replied.

So Jesus told all the people to sit down on the ground. Then he took the seven loaves, thanked God for them, and broke them into pieces. He gave them to his disciples, who distributed the bread to the crowd. A few small fish were found, too, so Jesus also blessed these and told the disciples to distribute them.

They ate as much as they wanted. Afterward, the disciples picked up seven large baskets of leftover food. There were about 4,000 men in the crowd that day,

> and Jesus sent them home after they had eaten. Immediately after this, he got into a boat with his disciples and crossed over to the region of Dalmanutha.
> (Mark 8:1–10)

IT'S SO FASCINATING to observe that as the disciples returned from their ministry tour, Jesus welcomed them and encouraged them to come away to a quiet place and rest awhile. He was helping them to set the rhythms of life and leadership they would need to embrace in order to stay strong for the long haul.

As in any of our best laid leadership plans, the crowds showed up. Jesus took compassion on them, and later in the day the disciples expressed their concern about their remote location. There was a need for the people to eat and the disciples asked Him to send the people away. I'm sure they had a concern for the physical needs of the people, but they were also concerned for themselves.

Jesus had just been modelling the rhythms of leadership when those plans went awry, and then disciples came up with an idea for how to get some downtime. So what does their leader do? Jesus throws them for a loop when He encourages them to feed the crowds themselves.

What would you have said? "Jesus, You're being unreasonable. What are we to feed them with? It would take more time than we have to earn the money needed to feed everyone, never mind the actual time it would take to feed them."

As their leader, Jesus heard what they said. Perhaps He understood that although a miracle was no new thing to Him, it truly was new to the disciples. They had just cast out demons and yet they hadn't considered that perhaps multiplying food was also within the realm of possibility.

And so Jesus included them in the miracle by asking them to see how much bread was available in the crowd. When they came back with five loaves and two fishes, Jesus brought order to what could have been chaos by focusing on what was most needful in the moment.

Again He included the disciples, asking them to have the crowd sit in groups of fifty or one hundred. He demonstrated His dependence on His Father as He looked to heaven and broke the bread and fishes into pieces to be distributed.

And to everyone's amazement, after serving everyone in the crowd of five thousand, there were leftovers.

Apart from the amazing miracle, this story demonstrates how Jesus as a leader invested in and empowered His disciples.

KALEIDOSCOPE REFLECTIONS

1. Jot down the leadership actions Jesus takes in this story.

2. Stop and reflect on a situation you find yourself in as a leader that seems too big and feels impossible. How can you take those leadership actions you named and make them work in your own situation?

3. Who are you going to share this story with and pursue a leadership conversation with? Be sure to record the Aha! moments you have together.

CHAPTER THIRTY-EIGHT
CHALLENGING SCARCITY MINDSETS

But the disciples had forgotten to bring any food. They had only one loaf of bread with them in the boat. As they were crossing the lake, Jesus warned them, "Watch out! Beware of the yeast of the Pharisees and of Herod."

At this they began to argue with each other because they hadn't brought any bread. Jesus knew what they were saying, so he said, "Why are you arguing about having no bread? Don't you know or understand even yet? Are your hearts too hard to take it in? 'You have eyes—can't you see? You have ears—can't you hear?' Don't you remember anything at all? When I fed the 5,000 with five loaves of bread, how many baskets of leftovers did you pick up afterward?"

"Twelve," they said.

"And when I fed the 4,000 with seven loaves, how many large baskets of leftovers did you pick up?"

"Seven," they said.

"Don't you understand yet?" he asked them.

(Mark 8:14–21)

OVER THE YEARS, I've sat in various finance meetings when the current reality is pressing in, demanding change. I've often been intrigued by the scarcity mindset in people who jump to cut the budget to solve the financial crunch. Who will we let go? What expenditures aren't necessary?

I often wonder about training our minds, hearts, ears, and eyes to shift our focus and ask:

- Whose viewpoint or perspective are we missing?
- What information are we missing?
- What is our mission, vision, and values and what do they demand?
- Where might we have gotten off-track in where we're spending our money?

In a particularly pressing situation we found ourselves in, our finances were tight—and the largest expenditure was the staff. As those large numbers stood out, our eyes turned there. Cutting staff became the focus of the cuts and we let go off a new hire.

When these situations are ill managed or the people involved lead poorly, the financial impacts are influential. When they occur, a scarcity mindset prevails. A crisis situation leads to looking for a crisis solution—which means that we focus on cutbacks over efficiency and relationship.

As I read this passage, it also makes me think of the commonalities of parenting and leadership. There are many moments when you think you've passed on information clearly, sure that everyone has learned and remembered what you told them. But that's not always the case.

In the mad scramble of that morning, imagine that the disciples forgot their lunch. Not only did they forget their lunch, but they forgot the abundance mindset of their leader. They lost sight of the fact that surely He could feed the twelve of them, if He could feed five thousand people from five loaves and two fishes and have leftovers.

When we look to Jesus as our leader, we operate in a very different sphere of leadership. It's a sphere of abundance, a sphere where what's needed will be provided. It's a sphere that is led by an ever-faithful God.

What is pressing in on you in leadership that you've allowed yourself to think too small about?

KALEIDOSCOPE REFLECTIONS

1. In what way is your outlook too small and hindering what could be?

2. How does the fear of not having enough cloud your view of God and His great abundance?

3. What is within your power to consider, change, and move forward with in order to get unstuck from a scarcity mindset?

CHAPTER THIRTY-NINE
RELATIONAL PING PONG

Then they reached Jericho, and as Jesus and his disciples left town, a large crowd followed him. A blind beggar named Bartimaeus (son of Timaeus) was sitting beside the road. When Bartimaeus heard that Jesus of Nazareth was nearby, he began to shout, "Jesus, Son of David, have mercy on me!"
"Be quiet!" many of the people yelled at him.
But he only shouted louder, "Son of David, have mercy on me!"
When Jesus heard him, he stopped and said, "Tell him to come here."
So they called the blind man. "Cheer up," they said. "Come on, he's calling you!" Bartimaeus threw aside his coat, jumped up, and came to Jesus.
"What do you want me to do for you?" Jesus asked.
"My Rabbi," the blind man said, "I want to see!"
And Jesus said to him, "Go, for your faith has healed you." Instantly the man could see, and he followed Jesus down the road.

(Mark 10:46–52)

WHEN JESUS IS a part of our lives, or even on the periphery of our lives, we come to experience a different kind of relationship with Him.

In this story of blind Bartimaeus, we often focus on the miracle of Bartimaeus receiving his sight. What if we looked at how that even came to be?

Jesus and the disciples had just reached Jericho. As Bartimaeus sat beside the road, he became aware that Jesus of Nazareth was nearby. He couldn't see, but he certainly could call out—and he did.

Here's the sequence of events as they happened.

- Bartimaeus called out to Jesus.
- The crowds told him to be quiet.
- Bartimaeus called out to Jesus.
- Jesus told him to come to Him.
- The crowd told him to go to Jesus.
- Bartimaeus came to Jesus.
- Jesus asked him what He could do for him.
- Bartimaeus said he wanted to see.
- Jesus told Bartimaeus to go because his faith had healed him.
- Bartimaeus followed Jesus down the road.

This is what I call relational ping pong. Our relationship with Jesus isn't one-way. It's a healthy back-and-forth, although not always an easy back-and-forth. We reach out, Jesus asks us to do something, and usually we're faced with an opportunity to obey.

Jesus meets us where we're at and longs to draw us to where we could be. He honours our pace, our way of being, and our situations. He approaches us and waits for us. He invites us and anticipates our response. He makes an offer to us and holds His hands out in an open gesture to us.

How will you bat the ball back in response to Him?

KALEIDOSCOPE REFLECTIONS

1. Take a moment to think about your relationship with Jesus. How would you describe it? What metaphor would you use?

2. When you see how Bartimaeus and Jesus related back and forth, can you relate that to:
   a) the ease and intimacy of your relationship with your leader and guide, Jesus? Describe what that looks like.
   b) how you work with your staff or your volunteers? Reflect on these relationships and what shifts you could make to be a more effective relational leader.

PART EIGHT
POWERFUL STORYTELLING

> Tell me the story of Jesus, write on my heart every word, tell me the stories most precious, sweetest than ever was heard.[26]
>
> —Fanny J. Crosby

THE GOSPELS REVEAL to us the power of story to teach, educate, move hearts to truth, stir our beliefs, and challenge our assumptions and even traditions.

Jesus was the master storyteller. He knew how to give a most excellent Ted Talk before any person had thought about that concept. He was countercultural. Jesus loved to leave the crowd with questions and wonderment at what He had just said, to huddle with His disciples to explore His teaching and see how those same teachings had the power to change lives. He wanted His disciples to understand this, because they would be the ones left to carry on to spread the good news of the Kingdom.

Long before the written word, stories have been our legacy of history, with one generation passing them on to another generation. Jesus knew the power of story to capture the attention and hearts of people.

Let's look in on Jesus and the power of story.

---

[26] Fanny J. Crosby, *Crowning Glory Hymnal* (Grand Rapids, MI: Zondervan, 1967), 357.

As believers in Jesus Christ, we are privileged to be a part of His great story. To be the carriers of His story, to carry it personally and as a body of believers in the way we chose to live our lives. Our lives often proclaim our Jesus story more loudly and accurately than words. And yet we are also responsible to know when and how to speak of our relationship with Jesus and what He invites everyone into.

CHAPTER FORTY
STORYTELLING

Once again Jesus began teaching by the lakeshore. A very large crowd soon gathered around him, so he got into a boat. Then he sat in the boat while all the people remained on the shore. He taught them by telling many stories in the form of parables, such as this one:

"Listen! A farmer went out to plant some seed. As he scattered it across his field, some of the seed fell on a footpath, and the birds came and ate it. Other seed fell on shallow soil with underlying rock. The seed sprouted quickly because the soil was shallow. But the plant soon wilted under the hot sun, and since it didn't have deep roots, it died. Other seed fell among thorns that grew up and choked out the tender plants so they produced no grain. Still other seeds fell on fertile soil, and they sprouted, grew, and produced a crop that was thirty, sixty, and even a hundred times as much as had been planted!" Then he said, "Anyone with ears to hear should listen and understand."

Later, when Jesus was alone with the twelve disciples and with the others who were gathered around, they asked him what the parables meant.

He replied, "You are permitted to understand the secret of the Kingdom of God. But I use parables for everything I say to outsiders, so that the Scriptures might be fulfilled: 'When they see what I do, they will learn nothing. When they hear what I say, they will not understand. Otherwise, they will turn to me and be forgiven.'"

Then Jesus said to them, "If you can't understand the meaning of this parable, how will you understand all the other parables? The farmer plants seed by taking God's word to others. The seed that fell on the footpath represents those who hear the message, only to have Satan come at once and take it away. The seed on the rocky soil represents those who hear the message and immediately receive it with joy. But since they don't have deep roots, they don't last long. They fall away as soon as they have problems or are persecuted for believing God's word. The seed that fell among the thorns represents others who hear God's word, but all too quickly

the message is crowded out by the worries of this life, the lure of wealth, and the desire for other things, so no fruit is produced. And the seed that fell on good soil represents those who hear and accept God's word and produce a harvest of thirty, sixty, or even a hundred times as much as had been planted!"
(Mark 4:1–20)[27]

MARK 4:1–34 RECORDS three parables and an explanation for another parable:

- The Four Soils
- The Explanation of the Parable of the Four Soils
- The Parable of the Growing Seed
- The Parable of the Mustard Seed

Our focus isn't on the parables themselves, but on how and why Jesus taught the people. Read these stories with the eye and heart of a teacher who wants His students to be willing. He wants them to learn to be willing to listen, willing to understand, willing to apply the truths given, and willing to grow and change. He wanted those who believed to understand more and those who chose not to believe to be left without true perception of His teachings.

I believe that His purpose in teaching the crowds was to create curiosity and thirst for more understanding. Then they would come back for more. His time with His disciples was to ensure that they understood and embraced His teaching so they could go out and spread the message by their lives and words.

Here we find ourselves at another lakeshore with crowds so great that Jesus had to step into a boat and push out from land before He began to speak. He taught the people by telling them stories, such as the story of the four soils, which He ended by saying to them, "Listening and understanding should happen if you are willing to hear."

Later, when Jesus was alone with the twelve disciples and the others who were gathered, they wanted to know what His stories meant. He explained to them that they were being given an understanding to the secret of the Kingdom of God.

---

[27] See also Mark 4:21–34, Matthew 13:1–9, and Luke 8:4–8.

Yet despite hearing His words, many still didn't understand what He said. This meant that they wouldn't recognize or acknowledge their sins—and it meant they wouldn't be forgiven. Jesus wondered aloud with them, "How are you ever going to understand all that I'm going to tell you if you don't understand these?"

Jesus made it plain that anyone who is willing to hear should sit up, listen, and understand. Be sure to pay attention to what you hear. The more you do, this the more you will understand.

This is a beautiful promise: those who open up to Jesus's teaching will be given more understanding. And it's a dire warning for those who don't listen: even the understanding they have will be taken away from them.

Jesus constantly used similar stories and illustrations to teach people as much as they were able to understand. When He taught, they were given the opportunity to seek understanding. In fact, in His public teaching He teaches only with parables. Afterward, when He was alone with His disciples, He explained the meaning of those parables to them. The disciples were given the opportunity to hear more, understand more, and discern more for themselves and their followers.

KALEIDOSCOPE REFLECTIONS

1. To be a great teacher, you must be a great learner. Do you agree or disagree? Why? What does this mean to you?

2. List a number of the teaching principles Jesus used. For each principle, see if you can figure out why Jesus taught this way.

3. Which of these principles significantly influenced the way you teach people?

4. Which principle is the most meaningful to you as consider the areas you teach in. Why?

5. How are you going to integrate this into your teaching style?

CHAPTER FORTY-ONE
MEANINGFUL ILLUSTRATIONS

Then Jesus began teaching them with stories: "A man planted a vineyard. He built a wall around it, dug a pit for pressing out the grape juice, and built a lookout tower. Then he leased the vineyard to tenant farmers and moved to another country. At the time of the grape harvest, he sent one of his servants to collect his share of the crop. But the farmers grabbed the servant, beat him up, and sent him back empty-handed. The owner then sent another servant, but they insulted him and beat him over the head. The next servant he sent was killed. Others he sent were either beaten or killed, until there was only one left—his son whom he loved dearly. The owner finally sent him, thinking, 'Surely they will respect my son.'

"But the tenant farmers said to one another, 'Here comes the heir to this estate. Let's kill him and get the estate for ourselves!' So they grabbed him and murdered him and threw his body out of the vineyard.

"What do you suppose the owner of the vineyard will do?" Jesus asked. "I'll tell you—he will come and kill those farmers and lease the vineyard to others. Didn't you ever read this in the Scriptures? 'The stone that the builders rejected has now become the cornerstone. This is the Lord's doing, and it is wonderful to see.'"

The religious leaders wanted to arrest Jesus because they realized he was telling the story against them—they were the wicked farmers. But they were afraid of the crowd, so they left him and went away.

Later the leaders sent some Pharisees and supporters of Herod to trap Jesus into saying something for which he could be arrested. "Teacher," they said, "we know how honest you are. You are impartial and don't play favorites. You teach the way of God truthfully. Now tell us—is it right to pay taxes to Caesar or not? Should we pay them, or shouldn't we?"

Jesus saw through their hypocrisy and said, "Why are you trying to trap me? Show me a Roman coin, and I'll tell you." When they handed it to him, he asked, "Whose picture and title are stamped on it?"

"Caesar's," they replied.

"Well, then," Jesus said, "give to Caesar what belongs to Caesar, and give to God what belongs to God."

His reply completely amazed them.

(Mark 12:1–17)

JESUS WAS A master at meeting people where they were at and speaking to them from what they understood. He often used meaningful illustrations and stories to help them see that which they hadn't understood before.

It's easy to tell someone to do this or that and then find that they are compliant. Jesus had a different perspective. He sought to engage their minds and hearts to create space for deeper understanding and growth.

Tending a vineyard was common in this region. They understood what it took to run a vineyard, hire help, get the job done, and pay employees. They understood the power of trust between servant and overseer.

And so Jesus fleshed out the story of a farmer. He got His point across so well that the religious leaders wanted to arrest Him right away, because they recognized themselves in the story and didn't want to hear any more.

That was the choice Jesus liked to leave people with. When they saw themselves, what were they going to do with this new knowledge? Jesus made them think, and in thinking they were given a choice.

Jesus knew that illustrations have the power to allow us to take a thought outside ourselves and in so doing see ourselves more clearly.

Read this passage through several times. Think about the power of story to capture people's imagination, to engage in the story because they recognize themselves. Then they can take a step of commitment.

A senior pastor I once knew was an amazing storyteller. One day he told a story of a time when he had been on his way out the door and couldn't find his keys. He checked coat pockets and drawers, then reverted to speaking to his wife and son in a way that sounded a lot like blaming them for misplacing his keys.

He spoke of the emotional tension and his choice to take a walk to the mailbox to cool down and see if he'd left his keys there. As he turned to home, he felt inner conflict over how he'd treated his wife and son.

While walking up the hill, he placed his hands in the pocket of his front sweatshirt—and there he found his keys.

In that moment, I was captured. I felt ready to hear the rest of the story. I could relate to thinking I knew something only to be proved wrong. This man had been proven wrong, but then he had acknowledged it, dealt with it, and he was free to move on.

This story let me know that I too could feel the freedom to move on. I could do this.

KALEIDOSCOPE REFLECTIONS

1. Think about some work that you want to inspire and have your people fully engage in. Think about your people and what they're familiar with. Think of a way to present the concept through a story or meaningful illustration that could draw them in.

2. Perhaps you're not a storyteller. Consider who on your team could rise to this creative challenge.

3. For example, you may want to tell a story that represents the principle of resiliency. Search for that term online. If resiliency brings a certain concept to mind, such as inner strength, search for that concept.

4. How could you be more in tune with meeting your people where they're at, engaging them in your mission, and creating space for them to be highly successful?

CHAPTER FORTY-TWO
EMBEDDING THE LEARNING

As Jesus was starting out on his way to Jerusalem, a man came running up to him, knelt down, and asked, "Good Teacher, what must I do to inherit eternal life?"

"Why do you call me good?" Jesus asked. "Only God is truly good. But to answer your question, you know the commandments: 'You must not murder. You must not commit adultery. You must not steal. You must not testify falsely. You must not cheat anyone. Honor your father and mother.'"

"Teacher," the man replied, "I've obeyed all these commandments since I was young."

Looking at the man, Jesus felt genuine love for him. "There is still one thing you haven't done," he told him. "Go and sell all your possessions and give the money to the poor, and you will have treasure in heaven. Then come, follow me."

At this the man's face fell, and he went away sad, for he had many possessions.

Jesus looked around and said to his disciples, "How hard it is for the rich to enter the Kingdom of God!" This amazed them. But Jesus said again, "Dear children, it is very hard to enter the Kingdom of God. In fact, it is easier for a camel to go through the eye of a needle than for a rich person to enter the Kingdom of God!"

The disciples were astounded. "Then who in the world can be saved?" they asked.

Jesus looked at them intently and said, "Humanly speaking, it is impossible. But not with God. Everything is possible with God."

Then Peter began to speak up. "We've given up everything to follow you," he said.

"Yes," Jesus replied, "and I assure you that everyone who has given up house or brothers or sisters or mother or father or children or property, for my sake and for the Good News, will receive now in return a hundred times as many houses, brothers, sisters, mothers, children, and property—along with persecution. And in

> the world to come that person will have eternal life. But many who are the greatest now will be least important then, and those who seem least important now will be the greatest then."
>
> They were now on the way up to Jerusalem, and Jesus was walking ahead of them. The disciples were filled with awe, and the people following behind were overwhelmed with fear. Taking the twelve disciples aside, Jesus once more began to describe everything that was about to happen to him. "Listen," he said, "we're going up to Jerusalem, where the Son of Man will be betrayed to the leading priests and the teachers of religious law. They will sentence him to die and hand him over to the Romans. They will mock him, spit on him, flog him with a whip, and kill him, but after three days he will rise again."
>
> (Mark 10:17–34)

EMBEDDING LEARNING USUALLY comes with some form of action that supports the information being imparted. As we read this passage, we continue to see Jesus's heart and mind. He knew and was prepared in each situation.

In this story, Jesus and the rich man's conversation starts with a question from the rich man, which Jesus replied to with another question. Then He provided the information the rich man was looking for. When someone speaks to us, asking questions often creates a greater level of engagement.

Asking curious questions are those filled with wonder and innocence. Curiosity, expressed in a childlike way, can change a judgmental question to one that says, "Help me understand" from a heart that truly wants to hear, listen, and understand.

A dear mentor of mine often said, "Don't put in someone's ear something you can bring out of their mouth." Engage the mind and create fertile soil for understanding and growth.

The rich man's response to this information held a measure of defensiveness and resistance. Jesus met him at his point of resistance and made an even bigger ask, which created space for deeper and more transformative learnings.

The rich man's response was to walk away with sadness. As an influential and caring leader, Jesus continued the conversation with His amazed disciples.

Go back and reread the passage by putting yourself in Jesus's place, the place of a leader who knew what God's purposes for Him were.

Reflect on how the conversation with the rich man unfolded. As this man walked away, Jesus turned to His disciples to debrief and help them understand a truth they found astonishing: it is in what we give up to fully embrace Jesus that makes the difference, not what we bring to give Him.

This truth was reinforced as they watched Jesus interact with the rich man. They saw Jesus's love for the man, and then again as He sat and talked with them in their state of astonishment.

KALEIDOSCOPE REFLECTIONS

1. Jot down what you know to be Jesus's purpose here on the earth.

2. Describe the give and take in the conversation. What do you glean about Jesus's purpose, outlook, attitude, and desired outcome from this conversation?

3. Describe a conversation you've held recently, or you need to have, in which you could overlay these learnings in order to become increasingly effective.

4. As you ponder this story, in what ways do you experience a shift in your thinking about transformational conversations?

CHAPTER FORTY-THREE
INVITE CONFLICT AS A TOOL FOR LEARNING

Later, as Jesus was teaching the people in the Temple, he asked, "Why do the teachers of religious law claim that the Messiah is the son of David? For David himself, speaking under the inspiration of the Holy Spirit, said, 'The Lord said to my Lord, Sit in the place of honor at my right hand until I humble your enemies beneath your feet.' Since David himself called the Messiah 'my Lord,' how can the Messiah be his son?" The large crowd listened to him with great delight.

Jesus also taught: "Beware of these teachers of religious law! For they like to parade around in flowing robes and receive respectful greetings as they walk in the marketplaces. And how they love the seats of honor in the synagogues and the head table at banquets. Yet they shamelessly cheat widows out of their property and then pretend to be pious by making long prayers in public. Because of this, they will be more severely punished."

Jesus sat down near the collection box in the Temple and watched as the crowds dropped in their money. Many rich people put in large amounts. Then a poor widow came and dropped in two small coins.

Jesus called his disciples to him and said, "I tell you the truth, this poor widow has given more than all the others who are making contributions. For they gave a tiny part of their surplus, but she, poor as she is, has given everything she had to live on."

(Mark 12:35–44)

SO OFTEN WE'RE afraid to enter into conversational conflict. And if we're honest with ourselves, our fear comes from our fear of being wrong. When this is our focus, our pride has taken up residence; we have started with the belief that there is a right and a wrong.

Our first focus should be on a curious approach and seeking to discover the facts, realizing that we don't know what we don't know. You may push back here and say, "But this is where we differ from Jesus, who was fully human and fully God." After all, Jesus had the advantage of being able to call on more than His human understanding.

We have the privilege to ask questions too. If Jesus who had full understanding asked questions, can we learn to as well?

An added blessing for us is that when Jesus left this earth, He left His Holy Spirit to convict us of sin and righteousness, to teach us and remind us of all things, to bestow His gifts on us and bless us with the fruit of His Spirit. We have access to the wisdom and ways of God through the wisdom and power of the Holy Spirit.

In some conversations, your emotions may tell you that there's only one right way—and you happen to know what it is. These are moments in which to pause and take a deep breath before entering the dialogue. This is where we need to recognize with a spirit of humility that we are far from knowing it all. In this way we are freed to invite another perspective to enrich us.

In this particular story, in the midst of Jesus's teaching He veers off in a direction that invites conflict. Inviting conflict is a useful yet risky tool. The benefit of this strategy to bring clarity is that you prepare yourself to remain in a state from which you can walk the full conversation through without being caught off-guard.

This is where you might argue again that Jesus had an advantage as the Son of God. I would love to know who stayed around for the follow-up conversation. Or did Jesus just quietly walk closer to the collection box and focus on an entirely lifegiving moment of truth?

This makes me ponder what else we can learn about how to handle situations in which we choose to stay with the conflict. When do we walk away and when do we stay present?

Developing a philosophy of conflict is a helpful tool. It takes time to come to understand yourself, what sets you off, and what your innate response to conflict is. You have to know what's most important and how to blend the various perspectives. It means bringing together what the organization stands for, what your perspective is, and what the other perspectives are. It means finding a space in which you can agree to the path forward together.

KALEIDOSCOPE REFLECTIONS

1. Stop and reflect on your philosophy of conflict. Describe it.

2. If you don't have a healthy conflict philosophy, jot down some bullet points on what you would like it to look like—apart from it being eradicated entirely.

3. Pay attention to how strong conflict resolution tools addresses our inner conflict. Handling your inner and outer conflict increases your leadership effectiveness.

CHAPTER FORTY-FOUR
TEACHABLE MOMENTS

Jesus sat down near the collection box in the Temple and watched as the crowds dropped in their money. Many rich people put in large amounts. Then a poor widow came and dropped in two small coins.

Jesus called his disciples to him and said, "I tell you the truth, this poor widow has given more than all the others who are making contributions. For they gave a tiny part of their surplus, but she, poor as she is, has given everything she had to live on."

(Mark 12:41–44)[28]

IN JUST A few verses, we catch a lot about Jesus as a leader. He's a leader who pays attention, is mindful, is aware of others, and embraces teachable moments.

Jesus took what was a small moment in time to read the crowd and help His disciples understand the true meaning of generosity. He paid attention to what others were doing from a non-judgmental stance, and also from a curious and learning stance.

This is crucial as a leader. These are opportunities for us to become masters of understanding people and the principles that drive them. By being curious bystanders, we gain a greater understanding of people and their ways. This matters because people are our ultimate work. Our leadership rises and falls on the health of our relationships and our ability to influence people in a positive direction.

---

[28] See also Luke 21:1–4.

Jesus used a meaager gift and a poor widow to teach His disciples a huge lesson. God's applause doesn't rest in the amount we give. Instead it's found in the measurement of how much we have versus what we purposefully give back to God. He is deserving of our all, not just a portion of it.

Teachable moments are all around us, from talking about the intricacies of a snowflake and God's great love to the recognition that in another circumstance God may have prevented an untimely accident. At another time, by the very design of the sky, He assures us of His presence even when our hearts are breaking. Watch and wait for His love and grace in the midst of daily life. Embrace and revel in it.

KALEIDOSCOPE REFLECTIONS

1. Take a stab at defining a teachable moment in a way that resonates with you. What are some of the qualities of that moment that make it effective?

2. Describe what you could do in the next week to increase your ability to be more aware of teachable moments and make use of them.

3. How will you use this lesson to increase the awareness of your people to develop in this area?

PART NINE
EMOTIONAL INTELLIGENCE

No creature can fly with just one wing. Gifted leadership occurs when heart and head—feeling and thought—meet. These are the two wings that allow a leader to soar.[29]

—Daniel Goleman, Richard Boyatzis, and Annie McKee

AUTHOR DANIEL GOLEMAN made emotional intelligence understandable and real to the everyday person. As I read his work back in the late 1990s, I felt inspired, affirmed, and excited for what this body of work could mean in learning to combine facts and emotions in a way that brought about greater understanding and more significant results.

Emotional intelligence is the ability to become more cognizant and versatile in using self-awareness, awareness of others, social awareness, and relational leadership to move forward. It allows for creating space not only for ourselves but for others. In so doing, we bring others with intention to the table and participate fully in creating healthy leadership spaces and outcomes.

---

[29] Daniel Goleman, Richard Boyatzis, and Annie McKee, *Unleashing the Power of Emotional Intelligence* (Boston, MA: Harvard Business School Press, 2002), 26.

CHAPTER FORTY-FIVE
HARD HEARTS ARE CHALLENGED

Immediately after this, Jesus insisted that his disciples get back into the boat and head across the lake to Bethsaida, while he sent the people home. After telling everyone good-bye, he went up into the hills by himself to pray.

Late that night, the disciples were in their boat in the middle of the lake, and Jesus was alone on land. He saw that they were in serious trouble, rowing hard and struggling against the wind and waves. About three o'clock in the morning Jesus came toward them, walking on the water. He intended to go past them, but when they saw him walking on the water, they cried out in terror, thinking he was a ghost. They were all terrified when they saw him.

But Jesus spoke to them at once. "Don't be afraid," he said. "Take courage! I am here!" Then he climbed into the boat, and the wind stopped. They were totally amazed, for they still didn't understand the significance of the miracle of the loaves. Their hearts were too hard to take it in.

After they had crossed the lake, they landed at Gennesaret. They brought the boat to shore and climbed out. The people recognized Jesus at once, and they ran throughout the whole area, carrying sick people on mats to wherever they heard he was. Wherever he went—in villages, cities, or the countryside—they brought the sick out to the marketplaces. They begged him to let the sick touch at least the fringe of his robe, and all who touched him were healed.

(Mark 6:45–56)

PERHAPS WHEN YOU saw this passage, you thought, *Oh, I know this story. It's about Jesus walking on the water.* And you would be correct.

Once again, we want to change our focus. We start by recognizing that Jesus had just finished feeding five thousand people in the most miraculous way. He then sent all the people away and had the disciples row Him across the lake. He was done.

He needed a fill up, and so He went by Himself into the hills to chat with His Father. It was late at night when the disciples went out to the middle of the lake.

As Jesus watched them from dry land, He recognized that they were in trouble. The storm was fierce and they were putting their best effort into staying alive. Jesus then got up from His seat on the sand and walked out onto the water, intending to walk right by the disciples.

This is a picture of a calm and seasoned leadership mindset. Jesus didn't rush to rescue His beloved disciples when He observed their struggle. His intent was to walk by.

Think about this! Our natural instinct as leaders is to rescue and get things fixed so we can move on. A strong lesson we learn from Jesus is that fixing the situation isn't the priority; the priority is for the people to grow and develop in their heart and character. In fact, becoming more like Jesus in the way we think, in our attitudes and actions, becomes our calling when we say we follow Jesus.

In the story, we also see a compassionate leader who was adaptable and ready for the moment.

But as Jesus got closer to His disciples, they screamed in terror. Not only was the weather awful, but now the spectre of a person walking on the water made them wonder if their eyes were playing tricks on them. Was this a ghost?

In His deep compassion for them, knowing they didn't get it, Jesus reached out to them to say, "Don't be afraid. Be courageous. I'm here." He didn't say any more; He simply climbed into the boat and the wind stopped.

Although they had just experienced the miracle of Jesus feeding five thousand people with five loaves and two fish, they were once again were amazed. They were amazed because their hearts were too hard to take it in.

It's interesting to read this as a leader who may have staff or volunteers who exhibit hard hearts. What a lesson it presents on how to work with our people when they have emotional baggage we wish they would just get over.

After a time of prayer with His Father, the story gives evidence of Jesus's ability to carry what His Father poured into Him and in turn pour wisdom, compassion, truth, and grace into the situation around Him.

The hard truth was their hard hearts. They hadn't learned, even as they were participants to amazing miracles. Jesus as their leader saw them, acknowledged them, and then chose His actions to help them get through and be part of the solution. He didn't jump in to fix their problem; He simply walked with them on the early leadership journey they lived together.

KALEIDOSCOPE REFLECTIONS

1. Reread this passage a few times and pay attention to what Jesus did. Although prayer may have been the starting point, what practical leadership actions do you see?

2. What do you think of Jesus's way of drawing near to the disciples and yet not jumping in right at the beginning to fix their situation? What leadership lessons do you see here?

3. What leadership situations have shown you the desperation of your people, and how have you handled it? What different actions might you need to acquire and use in similar situations?

4. Describe how you are walking with your leaders and what could be a meaningful shift in these relationships?

CHAPTER FORTY-SIX
HEATED EMOTIONS

When they returned to the other disciples, they saw a large crowd surrounding them, and some teachers of religious law were arguing with them. When the crowd saw Jesus, they were overwhelmed with awe, and they ran to greet him.

"What is all this arguing about?" Jesus asked.

One of the men in the crowd spoke up and said, "Teacher, I brought my son so you could heal him. He is possessed by an evil spirit that won't let him talk. And whenever this spirit seizes him, it throws him violently to the ground. Then he foams at the mouth and grinds his teeth and becomes rigid. So I asked your disciples to cast out the evil spirit, but they couldn't do it."

Jesus said to them, "You faithless people! How long must I be with you? How long must I put up with you? Bring the boy to me."

So they brought the boy. But when the evil spirit saw Jesus, it threw the child into a violent convulsion, and he fell to the ground, writhing and foaming at the mouth.

"How long has this been happening?" Jesus asked the boy's father.

He replied, "Since he was a little boy. The spirit often throws him into the fire or into water, trying to kill him. Have mercy on us and help us, if you can."

"What do you mean, 'If I can'?" Jesus asked. "Anything is possible if a person believes."

The father instantly cried out, "I do believe, but help me overcome my unbelief!"

When Jesus saw that the crowd of onlookers was growing, he rebuked the evil spirit. "Listen, you spirit that makes this boy unable to hear and speak," he said. "I command you to come out of this child and never enter him again!"

Then the spirit screamed and threw the boy into another violent convulsion and left him. The boy appeared to be dead. A murmur ran through the crowd as

> *people said, "He's dead." But Jesus took him by the hand and helped him to his feet, and he stood up.*
>
> *Afterward, when Jesus was alone in the house with his disciples, they asked him, "Why couldn't we cast out that evil spirit?"*
>
> *Jesus replied, "This kind can be cast out only by prayer."*
>
> *Leaving that region, they traveled through Galilee. Jesus didn't want anyone to know he was there, for he wanted to spend more time with his disciples and teach them. He said to them, "The Son of Man is going to be betrayed into the hands of his enemies. He will be killed, but three days later he will rise from the dead." They didn't understand what he was saying, however, and they were afraid to ask him what he meant.*
>
> (Mark 9:14–32)

IMAGINE THE EMOTIONS running rampant in this crowd.

There was the father who had watched his son be overcome time and again by an evil spirit seeking to destroy. The boy was no doubt riddled by fear, and the frustrated disciples were unable to do what they had been sent by Jesus to do. The large crowd, too, must have been frustrated with the disciples and religious leaders… and then overcome with awe when they saw Jesus. I have to wonder if the religious leaders were gloating at the disciples' inability to cast out the demon.

And how does Jesus handle this volatile situation when He arrives? He gets right to the point to discover what all the arguing is about. He listens to the explanation and sums it up with a measure of frustration at the unbelief He encounters. He asks for the disciples to bring Him the boy and again asks questions to the father for clarity. At this point, I think the father is at the end of his rope, his words holding both hope and doubt. Jesus picks up on the father's doubts as though they are a part of the solution.

Very quickly, the father gets it. He states his faith and acknowledges that he can't even believe without Jesus's help. There is such sweet vulnerability here in the midst of great agony.

Jonathon Edwards, a great American philosopher and revival preacher from the time of the Great American Awakening. knew this well. He is often quoted as having said,

> Nothing sets a person so much out of the devil's reach as humility, and so prepares the mind for true divine light without darkness,

and so clears the eye to look on things as they truly are... The meek will he guide in judgment. And the meek will he teach his way.[30]

Then Jesus does what He was sent to do. By the power of God, belief, and prayer, He casts out the evil spirit and lifts the young boy to life.

There is so much to discern from this story, so much to learn. As Jesus and the disciples huddle later away from the crowds, they ask the why-question: why couldn't they cast out the evil spirit? Jesus simply replies that prayer is the only way this kind can be cast out.

They then travel to Galilee where Jesus wants to spend more time with His disciples. He has information they don't understand, information which they fear.

This is when Jesus chooses to draw close to them. They're not at their best and may not realize how deeply they need Him now and for the days ahead.

As greater leadership influences are entrusted to you, you will discover your increased need to understand why you do what you do and how important it is to hear the stories of those you lead.

In knowing the stories of others in difficult situations, a space is created for us to become real and vulnerable, hearing each other, seeing each other, and appreciating the struggle we each face. In our humanity we can walk together to accomplish a common vision and reach a common destination.

KALEIDOSCOPE REFLECTIONS

1. How would you describe the way Jesus led in this situation and what He did?

2. Reflect on a highly emotional situation you've had to handle as a leader and examine your approach. Describe it.

---

[30] Jonathon Edwards, *Works of Jonathon Edwards, Volume One* (New Haven, CT: Yale University Press, 2009), 399.

3. What are some of the key leadership learnings from this story that would increase your ability to get through these kinds of highly emotive situations?

CHAPTER FORTY-SEVEN
HANGRY JESUS

The next morning as they were leaving Bethany, Jesus was hungry. He noticed a fig tree in full leaf a little way off, so he went over to see if he could find any figs. But there were only leaves because it was too early in the season for fruit. Then Jesus said to the tree, "May no one ever eat your fruit again!" And the disciples heard him say it.

(Mark 11:12–14)[31]

I LOVE THIS story! It shows us the humanity of Jesus.

When I experience frustration, it's so easy to excuse myself or create expectations of myself that I was never meant to bear. Here we see that Jesus was hungry. In this state, He saw a fig tree that was intended to bear fruit, but it only bore leaves. In fact, it was too early for the tree to bear fruit. Jesus's hunger affected His response, and in the hunger of that moment the fig tree was relegated to just being a leaf-bearing tree rather than a fruit-bearing tree.

Reading this causes me to ponder how we can have multiple responses to life and leadership when facing situations that frustrate us. Our personal situations and how we feel about them in the moment has the power to affect our response.

One of my leadership partners once challenged me with the following illustration. You need to hold your leadership like you would

---

[31] See also Matthew 21:18–22.

hold a bird in your outstretched hand. If you squeeze your fingers too tightly, you'll squeeze the life out of the bird. If you hold it too loosely, it'll fly away. Either way, you'll lose what you could have kept.

Jesus demonstrates for us here that there will be times we're pressed beyond measure, and we'll handle a situation out of our lesser selves, version of ourselves we don't want to be.

In this great time of conflict, Jesus, although frustrated, did not focus on a person; He focused on an object. The challenge for us is to not lay blame either on ourselves or others. We need to see ourselves and others in our humanity and respond with that in mind. Our role is to help them examine the situation, name the issue and invite those involved to step up to being a part of thee solution.

KALEIDOSCOPE REFLECTIONS

1. We can grasp what lies before us with a tight fist, squeezing the life from it. Describe what that looks like for you when you're in a frustrating leadership situation. Is there something you need to lessen your grip on? What is it? How might you do that? Why is this important for your ongoing influence?

2. Where aren't you holding your leadership responsibilities securely enough to thrive? Describe what that looks like for you when you're in a frustrating leadership position. Explain what you can do to ensure that you have a healthy hold on the situation. How can you develop that healthy leadership hold? Why is this important to your future influence?

CHAPTER FORTY-EIGHT
HANDLING STRESSFUL EMOTIONS

They were now on the way up to Jerusalem, and Jesus was walking ahead of them. The disciples were filled with awe, and the people following behind were overwhelmed with fear. Taking the twelve disciples aside, Jesus once more began to describe everything that was about to happen to him. "Listen," he said, "we're going up to Jerusalem, where the Son of Man will be betrayed to the leading priests and the teachers of religious law. They will sentence him to die and hand him over to the Romans. They will mock him, spit on him, flog him with a whip, and kill him, but after three days he will rise again."

(Mark 10:32–34)

PICTURE YOURSELF AS a disciple on this walk with Jesus. You're in awe, and as a person in the crowd with the disciples you're also filled with fear.

Jesus takes the disciples aside to be sure they understand what's about to come. I can imagine there was profound silence as Jesus's words sank in. He would be betrayed, sentenced to die, handed over to the Romans, mocked, spit on, flogged with a whip, and killed—and three days later, he would rise from the dead.

Put yourself in the place of one of the disciples, listening to this man they had chosen to follow. They'd heard His teachings, seen His miracles, and stood in awe of who He was. Now they were faced with the end of the story. Imagine the waves of emotion washing through them at this reminder.

Despite their tumultuous emotions, Jesus admonished them to listen. There was no opportunity to live in denial. He put the facts on the table, no matter how difficult they were. When facts are clear, we have the choice to navigate between how we feel and what we know to be true.

Self-awareness means that we're able to name our emotions and lead through them in a way that moves us forward. There are times when we want to run away from the way we feel. To navigate stressful emotional settings, though, we need to name the emotion, acknowledge its power, revisit the facts of the current reality, and choose how to use emotion and fact to move us forward.

In emotional intelligence terms, Jesus shows empathy over sympathy. Both empathy and sympathy start in the same space; they see the situation for what it is and choose to listen to the people involved. Sympathy then leaves people in a victim state where they don't think they can do anything. Empathy, on the other hand, allows people to acknowledge how they feel. From that place, they can figure out what to do to bring some value to the situation and help in the midst of it. With empathy, they're given the opportunity to rise to who they are called to be. Demonstrating empathy doesn't equate with fixing the situation. It means acknowledging the situation and recognizing its value in moving people forward in the face of overwhelming odds.

KALEIDOSCOPE REFLECTIONS

1. Take the time to stop and reflect about what makes a situation emotionally charged in the spaces where you lead.

2. Describe how you choose to handle situations and your people when emotions are running high.

3. How do you differentiate between being reactionary versus responsive?

4. Revisit a situation that was emotionally charged for you. What do you understand about it in light of this passage? How does this influence how you could deal with future emotionally charged situations?

5. Reflect on what you've learned about yourself and the way you've been empowered to move forward.

CHAPTER FORTY-NINE
EMOTIONS AND FACTS WORK TOGETHER

When Jesus returned to Capernaum several days later, the news spread quickly that he was back home. Soon the house where he was staying was so packed with visitors that there was no more room, even outside the door. While he was preaching God's word to them, four men arrived carrying a paralyzed man on a mat. They couldn't bring him to Jesus because of the crowd, so they dug a hole through the roof above his head. Then they lowered the man on his mat, right down in front of Jesus. Seeing their faith, Jesus said to the paralyzed man, "My child, your sins are forgiven."

But some of the teachers of religious law who were sitting there thought to themselves, "What is he saying? This is blasphemy! Only God can forgive sins!"

Jesus knew immediately what they were thinking, so he asked them, "Why do you question this in your hearts? Is it easier to say to the paralyzed man 'Your sins are forgiven,' or 'Stand up, pick up your mat, and walk'? So I will prove to you that the Son of Man has the authority on earth to forgive sins." Then Jesus turned to the paralyzed man and said, "Stand up, pick up your mat, and go home!"

And the man jumped up, grabbed his mat, and walked out through the stunned onlookers. They were all amazed and praised God, exclaiming, "We've never seen anything like this before!"

Then Jesus went out to the lakeshore again and taught the crowds that were coming to him. As he walked along, he saw Levi son of Alphaeus sitting at his tax collector's booth. "Follow me and be my disciple," Jesus said to him. So Levi got up and followed him.

Later, Levi invited Jesus and his disciples to his home as dinner guests, along with many tax collectors and other disreputable sinners. (There were many people of this kind among Jesus' followers.) But when the teachers of religious law who were Pharisees saw him eating with tax collectors and other sinners, they asked his disciples, "Why does he eat with such scum?"

> *When Jesus heard this, he told them, "Healthy people don't need a doctor—sick people do. I have come to call not those who think they are righteous, but those who know they are sinners."*
>
> (Mark 2:1–17)

MARK 2–3 PRESENTS many stories that normally lead us to focus on the miracles Jesus performed. Each story also carries with it the criticism He faced as He went about doing His Father's will. And in each story, we encounter descriptions that reveal Jesus's emotions and what He knew to be true. When you read these stories with your emotions, you sense only a bit of what Jesus in His humanity must have felt.

We also see that Jesus acted out of facts He knew to be true and also out of the reason He was sent to the earth. These stories reveal His humanity and divinity, His ability and willingness to work with both the emotions and facts. His Father's love and purpose for Him sustained and strengthened Him. Despite not having a divine nature, we too can learn to navigate the world of emotions and facts in order to authentically move forward.

Robert Southey, an English poet from the 1800s, once wrote, "Curses are like young chickens: they always come home to roost."[32] We often hear this interpreted as "the chickens will come home to roost," and it proves to be true time and again. It's an important concept and one that helps us lead through our emotions when we're falsely accused. Others can smear our reputation, but they cannot destroy our character. Our character is between ourselves and God and we have been given the power to live up to what we say we believe. We have the choice to submit to the Holy Spirit's work in us and grow in the fruit of His Spirit, which is our ultimate challenge or to remain just as we are.

Jesus had no legalistic formula for these situations. What He did have was a clear mandate which required Him to listen to His Father and have the courage to obey, no matter the consequences. This focus allowed Him to deal with often unfair and unjust criticism.

One of the best words of advice I received in my leadership journey was about asking for feedback, to be proactive in seeking others'

---

[32] Robert Southey, *The Curse of Kehama* (London, UK: Longman, Hurst, Rees, Orme and Brown, Paternoster-Row, 1810).

viewpoints so my heart would be prepared to hear what I needed to hear both in celebration and in caution. Criticism is painful, and learning how to deal with it is part of the leader's journey.

A dear friend and mentor advised me early on to be prepared to ask two questions of others so I could grow. By being proactive in asking these questions, I prepared myself to hear what was being said and make the most of it without a lot of emotional drama.

1. What do you want to celebrate about me and my leadership?
2. What cautions do you want to give to me about my leadership?

This can be used almost anywhere in our lives. All we have to do is replace the word leadership with parenting, teaching, attention to detail, and so on.

If you've ever faced criticism, then looking at the life of Jesus will help you find comfort, wisdom, courage, and direction for facing your critics with humility, clarity, and with a brave heart.

KALEIDOSCOPE REFLECTIONS

1. Describe your observations of what Jesus's emotional response might have been in the situations recorded.

2. Carefully examine how Jesus responded despite the potential for hurtful conflict.

3. How do the words of John 8:32—*"the truth will set you free"*—apply to these stories?

4. Reflect on the time in your life when you were falsely accused. How would you describe what you went through? How did it end? What did you learn? Is there anything left undone that could fester as a root of bitterness that should be addressed?

5. Who will you choose to ask questions of caution and celebration? Now do it, and then come back and talk about the experience.

PART TEN
OUR FRIEND, SAVIOUR, AND LEADER

> There is a name I love to hear,
>   I love to sing its worth;
>   It sounds like music in mine ear,
>   The sweetest name on earth.
> Oh, how I love Jesus,
> Oh, how I love Jesus,
> Oh, how I love Jesus,
> Because He first loved me![33]
>
> —Frederick Whitfield

JESUS, OH WHAT a Saviour we have who divested all of heaven's glory to come and be with us. Oh what a friend He is who chooses to walk with us, teach us, correct us, love us, and move us forward in His time and ways. Oh what a leader He was—not just a great role model, but one who had a real, authentic way of being and doing, showing Himself to us in His divinity and humanity. He came to set us free and empower us to be all we were created to be.

---

[33] Frederick Whitfield, *Crowning Glory Hymnal* (Grand Rapids, MI: Zondervan, 1967), 253.

CHAPTER FIFTY
EGO BLINDS TRUE PERSPECTIVE
AND LEAVES US EMPTY

Then James and John, the sons of Zebedee, came over and spoke to him. "Teacher," they said, "we want you to do us a favor."

"What is your request?" he asked.

They replied, "When you sit on your glorious throne, we want to sit in places of honor next to you, one on your right and the other on your left."

But Jesus said to them, "You don't know what you are asking! Are you able to drink from the bitter cup of suffering I am about to drink? Are you able to be baptized with the baptism of suffering I must be baptized with?"

"Oh yes," they replied, "we are able!"

Then Jesus told them, "You will indeed drink from my bitter cup and be baptized with my baptism of suffering. But I have no right to say who will sit on my right or my left. God has prepared those places for the ones he has chosen."

When the ten other disciples heard what James and John had asked, they were indignant. So Jesus called them together and said, "You know that the rulers in this world lord it over their people, and officials flaunt their authority over those under them. But among you it will be different. Whoever wants to be a leader among you must be your servant, and whoever wants to be first among you must be the slave of everyone else. For even the Son of Man came not to be served but to serve others and to give his life as a ransom for many."

(Mark 10:35–45)

THIS PASSAGE IS the lynchpin of our understanding of the type of leadership Jesus calls us to as His followers. And yet it is also a difficult passage, as it leads us to see and fight our egos and pride. It requires us to make a choice—to die to our selfish ambitions and come alive to all the possibilities found in faith in Jesus Christ. This is our opportunity to experience freedom and discover the fruit of God's Holy Spirit ever increasing in our lives.

The story starts with what seemed to be a pretty simple request by James and John. We also see that they lacked awareness of the consequences of their ask. If this request had been granted, it would have come with a bitter cup of suffering which they knew nothing of. This ask created division and indignation among the disciples.

Choosing to be a servant means that I need to understand what it looks like when I'm not being a servant. Below, I've outlined a powerful tool to better understand servanthood. For me, I had to understand what it looked like when I walked in pride, and what I needed to do to walk humbly with my God. I still grapple with this. These four mindsets, or ways of seeing life, have helped me to understand my own pride and to name it when it arises.

Mindset 1: I am superior. We know we're in the superior mindset when we get impatient with others, when we're frustrated, patronizing, or just plain disdainful. We feel like we have the right way in the right timing—and they just don't get it. It's all about us!

Mindset 2: I deserve. We know we're in the deserving mindset when we feel like we aren't getting what we deserve from others, or when we feel that they owe us or we find ourselves resentful. Again, we have become focused on ourselves. It's all about us!

Mindset 3: I must wear a mask. We know we're in the mask mindset when we feel anxious, afraid, needy, and overwhelmed. We struggle to let others see who we really are. It's stressful to keep on a game face when everything is falling apart. It's all about us!

Mindset 4: I am inadequate. We know we're in the inadequate mindset when we feel helpless, bitter, jealous, or depressed. In this state, we feel that we simply aren't good enough. We see ourselves as being inadequate compared to others. It's all about us!

The common denominator with all these mindsets is that we focus on ourselves, limiting our ability to see and comprehend clearly. We cannot see the humanity of others; instead we turn them into objects.

This allows us to justify ourselves, creating a space for us to judge others.

But there's a fifth mindset that allows us to gain perspective in relationship to ourselves, God, and others.

Mindset 5: You and I are equal in our humanity. We know we're equal in our humanity mindset when we can view ourselves as having worth, when we're able to be lifegiving. This allows us to view others as equal in their creation. They're worthy and deserving as people. They deserve to receive rhythms of grace and truth. I will feel peaceful, optimistic, realistic, and filled with expectancy, delight, gratitude, and warmth.

Not recognizing our emotions and how they affect us and our relationships with others gives space for our leadership perspective to enter a downward spiral. Many would say that pride or ego have a positive side, yet if the focus is on me then it will be too narrow. When we have a right-sized ego, it means we're confident and aware of our strengths and abilities, able to use them to serve a greater cause.

I know that the ability to live this way comes from a deep dependence and willingness to live in obedience to God.

KALEIDOSCOPE REFLECTIONS

1. As you consider the feelings and emotions represented by each face of pride, is there one you tend to wear more frequently?

2. In becoming more aware of these emotions, what is one thing you can do to shift your mindset when you first recognize an emotional trigger event?

3. How would you define the difference between pride, ego, and confidence? As you reflect on your behaviours, how are you displaying pride or ego in a harmful way, and how are you displaying confidence in a way that will move you forward?

4. Are there ways in which you display outward pride or ego because you lack inward confidence? What kind of dissonance does that create inside you?

5. Reflect on what Jesus said when He described how worldly leaders flaunt their authority and lord it over others. Then He challenged that among us it would be different. If you want to lead, learn to serve first. If you want to be first, learn to do that by serving. What would it look like for you to learn to live with a greater heart of service towards others?

CHAPTER FIFTY-ONE
WHO GETS THE GLORY

A man with leprosy came and knelt in front of Jesus, begging to be healed. "If you are willing, you can heal me and make me clean," he said.

Moved with compassion, Jesus reached out and touched him. "I am willing," he said. "Be healed!" Instantly the leprosy disappeared, and the man was healed. Then Jesus sent him on his way with a stern warning: "Don't tell anyone about this. Instead, go to the priest and let him examine you. Take along the offering required in the law of Moses for those who have been healed of leprosy. This will be a public testimony that you have been cleansed."

But the man went and spread the word, proclaiming to everyone what had happened. As a result, large crowds soon surrounded Jesus, and he couldn't publicly enter a town anywhere. He had to stay out in the secluded places, but people from everywhere kept coming to him.

(Mark 1:40–45)[34]

JESUS, THOUGH SON of God and Son of Man, saw no need to play the games of thinking "I'm better than you," "I'm less than you," "I'm entitled to…" and "I'm not going to let you see the real me." He was authentic and true to Himself, to His Father, and to His calling for His Father's glory and our edification.

In this story, Jesus came down from the mountain and entered a village. He was then approached by a man with leprosy who believed that Jesus could heal him if He wanted to.

---

[34] See also Matthew 8:1–4 and Luke 5:12–16.

Jesus wanted to and He did. He also admonished the man to go to the priest with the money he was required to pay for the healing and not tell anyone on the way.

However, the man healed from leprosy couldn't stay silent and so the word spread quickly, the crowds multiplied, and Jesus withdrew to the wilderness to pray.

Jesus was the new guy in town, attracting a lot of attention. Because of the awesome things He was doing, He could have bragged up a storm or had the people around Him spread the word, but He asked them not to.

One of the ways to find the greatest fulfillment in ministry is to know what has to be done, then do it without caring who gets the credit. It's not about me; it's all about Him.

See it. Do it. Share it.

Oh to be able to change a life by a simple touch. And yet we have that opportunity every time we're with others. We can submit to our Heavenly Father, lean into the power of the Holy Spirit, and allow God to reach out and touch others in ways we cannot preplan or even imagine.

KALEIDOSCOPE REFLECTIONS

1. When you're given the opportunity to do something outstanding, how do you handle the press that goes with it?

2. Is it easier to be humble when someone acknowledges your contribution, or when no one notices?

3. Do you want others to take note of what has been accomplished by you, the person who made it happen? Why?

CHAPTER FIFTY-TWO
WHEN LEADERSHIP LEADS TO DEATH, METAPHORICALLY OR IN REALITY

At dawn's first light, the high priests, with the religious leaders and scholars, arranged a conference with the entire Jewish Council. After tying Jesus securely, they took him out and presented him to Pilate.

Pilate asked him, "Are you the 'King of the Jews'?"

He answered, "If you say so." The high priests let loose a barrage of accusations.

Pilate asked again, "Aren't you going to answer anything? That's quite a list of accusations." Still, he said nothing. Pilate was impressed, really impressed.

It was a custom at the Feast to release a prisoner, anyone the people asked for. There was one prisoner called Barabbas, locked up with the insurrectionists who had committed murder during the uprising against Rome. As the crowd came up and began to present its petition for him to release a prisoner, Pilate anticipated them: "Do you want me to release the King of the Jews to you?" Pilate knew by this time that it was through sheer spite that the high priests had turned Jesus over to him.

But the high priests by then had worked up the crowd to ask for the release of Barabbas. Pilate came back, "So what do I do with this man you call King of the Jews?"

They yelled, "Nail him to a cross!"

Pilate objected, "But for what crime?"

But they yelled all the louder, "Nail him to a cross!"

Pilate gave the crowd what it wanted, set Barabbas free and turned Jesus over for whipping and crucifixion.

The soldiers took Jesus into the palace (called Praetorium) and called together the entire brigade. They dressed him up in purple and put a crown plaited from a thornbush on his head. Then they began their mockery: "Bravo, King of the Jews!" They banged on his head with a club, spit on him, and knelt down in mock worship. After they had had their fun, they took off the purple cape and put his own clothes back on him. Then they marched out to nail him to the cross.

There was a man walking by, coming from work, Simon from Cyrene, the father of Alexander and Rufus. They made him carry Jesus' cross.

The soldiers brought Jesus to Golgotha, meaning "Skull Hill." They offered him a mild painkiller (wine mixed with myrrh), but he wouldn't take it. And they nailed him to the cross. They divided up his clothes and threw dice to see who would get them.

They nailed him up at nine o'clock in the morning. The charge against him—the king of the jews—was scrawled across a sign. Along with him, they crucified two criminals, one to his right, the other to his left. People passing along the road jeered, shaking their heads in mock lament: "You bragged that you could tear down the Temple and then rebuild it in three days—so show us your stuff! Save yourself! If you're really God's Son, come down from that cross!"

The high priests, along with the religion scholars, were right there mixing it up with the rest of them, having a great time poking fun at him: "He saved others—but he can't save himself! Messiah, is he? King of Israel? Then let him climb down from that cross. We'll all become believers then!" Even the men crucified alongside him joined in the mockery.

At noon the sky became extremely dark. The darkness lasted three hours. At three o'clock, Jesus groaned out of the depths, crying loudly, "Eloi, Eloi, lama sabachthani?" which means, "My God, my God, why have you abandoned me?"

Some of the bystanders who heard him said, "Listen, he's calling for Elijah." Someone ran off, soaked a sponge in sour wine, put it on a stick, and gave it to him to drink, saying, "Let's see if Elijah comes to take him down."

But Jesus, with a loud cry, gave his last breath. At that moment the Temple curtain ripped right down the middle. When the Roman captain standing guard in front of him saw that he had quit breathing, he said, "This has to be the Son of God!"

There were women watching from a distance, among them Mary Magdalene, Mary the mother of the younger James and Joses, and Salome. When Jesus was in Galilee, these women followed and served him, and had come up with him to Jerusalem.

Late in the afternoon, since it was the Day of Preparation (that is, Sabbath eve), Joseph of Arimathea, a highly respected member of the Jewish Council, came. He was one who lived expectantly, on the lookout for the kingdom of God. Working up his courage, he went to Pilate and asked for Jesus' body. Pilate questioned whether he could be dead that soon and called for the captain to verify that he was really dead. Assured by the captain, he gave Joseph the corpse.

Having already purchased a linen shroud, Joseph took him down, wrapped him in the shroud, placed him in a tomb that had been cut into the rock, and rolled a large stone across the opening. Mary Magdalene and Mary, mother of Joses, watched the burial.

(Mark 15:1–47, MSG)

THIS PASSAGE MAKES me think about Jesus in ways I may have missed in the past. There are several sections to Mark 15:

1. Jesus's trial before Pilate.
2. Jesus being mocked by the soldiers who arrested Him.
3. Jesus's crucifixion.
4. Jesus's death.
5. Jesus's burial.

Jesus heals the sick, casts out demons, empowers the ordinary to do the extraordinary, and calms the storm. He feeds the multitudes, then eats supper with and even washes the feet of the one who betrays Him. He is then forsaken, rejected, bound, and falsely accused.

And He is silent before His accusers.

He is dead.

So much about Jesus's life goes against the grain of our egos. His birth? In a stable. His earthly parents? A carpenter and homemaker. His life? Spent with the least of these. His byline? To serve others. His death? Brutally crucified. His voice? Straightforward and offensive. His asks? Both hard and humbling.

Jesus was given as the greatest gift the world had ever seen. In our earthly mindset, we would expect pomp, splendour, respect, and power. What we see is humble beginnings, uncharacteristic growing up years, a brutal adulthood of ministry, and then betrayal and death.

I find silence hard. I find it hard even when there's nothing at stake. But when I'm accused, mocked, insulted, or threatened, I find that I want to defend myself and my motives. I want to lash out. I want to be right and prove the other person wrong.

For example, one day I came into work and heard my name being called. I looked across the hall and realized I was being summoned. I popped my head into the office to find that I was to appear before a grievance committee.

What? What was this about?

I was simply told that I would be notified when to come to the boardroom. It appeared that a group of volunteers had grievances towards me.

My heartrate sped up as I stepped out of that office. I found myself sputtering and fuming. My frustration grew, and my anger rose. I simply sat with all that until there were major shifts in my thinking and attitudes. I imagined Jesus silently facing His accusers. I knew this thought was a gift from God.

When I was called to attend this grievance meeting, I felt an unexplainable calm and a sense that this was my time to listen and remain silent. I was to learn what I didn't know.

The meeting convened and I sat as each volunteer had the opportunity to speak. My mind raced and the rush of my beating heart in my ears was loud. But my calm turned to curiosity. Why had no one called or emailed me? How had this gotten to such a state? What had I missed? How deep were the hurts that this had been escalated to this point?

The meeting concluded and the verdict was in. To my surprise—and I will say, confusion—I was vindicated, the volunteers chastised, and I still had no answers. And neither did the volunteers who sat around the table.

After that meeting, I was advised to avoid having conversations with these volunteers—but that advice didn't resonate with my heart. My mind reeled. If we couldn't talk and hear each other's stories, how were we to move forward?

It was a painful and emotional drive home. There had been no resolution, no oil of grace applied, no space for forgiveness and reconciliation provided.

Over the weeks to come, I ran to my heavenly Father's heart, to His Word. I processed, journaled, and poured out my learnings. I didn't want this painful season to be wasted.

These concepts helped to shape and mould me as a leader in the seasons to come. I also came to see gaps of unfinished thoughts and perhaps misunderstandings.

The following document is where I landed in these unchartered waters of leadership.

TEN PRINCIPLES FOR WORKING TOWARDS AN AGREEMENT OF UNITY IN THE CONTEXT OF COMMUNITY

1. The Principle of Affirmation (Ephesians 1:4, John 15:16). This principle goes beyond nice words:
- See the person as God sees them (Ephesians 1:4), including their talents, abilities, and gifts (John 15:16).
- Believe the best of each person and allow God's Spirit to care for the rest.

2. The Principle of Relationship (John 13:34–35). This principle reminds us to love with the power of Christ's love through you, no matter how you have been treated.

3. The Principle of Hurt (Hebrews 12:15). This principle admonishes us to know and address our hurts, then work it out with God and allow others to help us see clearly and deal with our own stuff.

4. The Principle of Choosing Words that Edify (Psalm 19:14, Proverbs 15:1, Proverbs 15:4). Our words to one another have the power to build up or to destroy.
- Prayerfully think through and choose the words you speak. Will your words make the situation worse or better? Grace must be balanced with truth.
- Clarify the issue that needs to be addressed. Is it organizational or personal? Choose to understand your emotions and deal with them separately. Invite others involved to express their perspective in a spirit of love and unity.

5. The Principle of God's Control (Hebrews 13:7–9). Learn to listen and trust God to hold your heart and mind for His greater purposes.

6. The Principle of Submission to Christ's Lordship (Philippians 2:5–8). Before you give any response:
- Seek God's wisdom (on the spot) by submitting to His leadership and direction.
- Major on the majors and minor on the minors.

- Suggest a possible solution.
- Invite dialogue.

7. **The Principle of Team Solutions** (1 Corinthians 1:10). Invite their solution. In light of their understanding, what would you suggest?

8. **The Principle of Agreement** (Luke 24:13–34). The story on the Emmaus Road illustrates the following:
    - The disciples discussed what they didn't understand.
    - Jesus entered the discussion. He brought admonition and knowledge.
    - Jesus gave them unity around Himself.
    - They then knew their next step.

9. **The Principle of Prayer** (Romans 8:26–30). Prayer is about making a commitment for God's purposes to be worked through both of you for the furtherance of His Kingdom.

This pain-filled story of mine made me feel like I wasn't being seen, heard, or respected, which led me to deep and profound learnings that moulded me for God's purposes. It made me see and hear Jesus in ways I hadn't understood before. It made me realize that although I wasn't dying physically, I was to die to my own selfish ways. For me, it was a metaphorical death.

This made me realize that Jesus is the man I want to follow. He literally faced death as He chose to lead His people.

Scripture describes Jesus literal death. With raw wounds, He stood as they dressed Him in purple, pressed a crown of thorns on His head, struck Him on the head with a reed stick, spit on Him, and mocked Him in false worship. When they got tired of their mockery, they once again dressed Him in His own clothes and led Him away to be crucified.

And yet in all of this, He remained silent.

If there was any grace, it was when they gave His cross to Simon of Cyrene to carry.

The drama continued as they offered to drug Him with myrrh, but He refused it. They pounded nails into His hands and feet. They gambled His clothes away and continued to call out and mock Him.

In the darkest hour of His life, He lifted His voice to the heavens and called out, *"Eloi, Eloi, lema sabachthani?"* This haunting cry breaks our hearts and troubles our minds, as Jesus cried out to His Father, *"My God, My God, why have you abandoned me?"* (Mark 15:34)

Then someone asked permission to bury the body of Jesus. Lovingly, Joseph of Arimathea brought linen to wrap the body of Jesus. He took Jesus's lifeless body down from the cross, wrapped it in the cloth, and laid it in a tomb which he sealed with a large stone.

This was the same Jesus who had walked into their lives and turned the world upside down. It was the same Jesus who had walked with, honoured, mentored, taught, and led them.

He was now dead.

They couldn't believe what they had seen and experienced. This was not the way they had thought the story would end. No longer would they sit at His feet to learn, to be affirmed, to be challenged, and to see the love flow from His heart to rest on them.

This is leadership personified. He is not only our great role model. He is so much more than that. He was and is the real essence of leadership. Everything He thought, everything He said, and everything He did flowed from the knowledge of who had sent Him and gave Him His purpose, to whom He would be returning very shortly.

And this was not the end.

KALEIDOSCOPE REFLECTIONS

1. As you read this passage with leadership eyes, what captures your heart most? Do you view Jesus as a leader and, perhaps, your leader?

2. What would it look like, or feel like, to be willing to give up your life for your people, actually dying for your people? Are you willing to do that? Describe what that would mean for you.

3. What would it look like, or feel like, to choose to live for your people. Are you willing to do that? Describe what that would mean for you.

4. Reflect on the ways this passage shifts your thinking about your role as a leader.

CHAPTER FIFTY-THREE
OUR SAVIOUR, LORD, LEADER, AND GUIDE

Saturday evening, when the Sabbath ended, Mary Magdalene, Mary the mother of James, and Salome went out and purchased burial spices so they could anoint Jesus' body. Very early on Sunday morning, just at sunrise, they went to the tomb. On the way they were asking each other, "Who will roll away the stone for us from the entrance to the tomb?" But as they arrived, they looked up and saw that the stone, which was very large, had already been rolled aside.

When they entered the tomb, they saw a young man clothed in a white robe sitting on the right side. The women were shocked, but the angel said, "Don't be alarmed. You are looking for Jesus of Nazareth, who was crucified. He isn't here! He is risen from the dead! Look, this is where they laid his body. Now go and tell his disciples, including Peter, that Jesus is going ahead of you to Galilee. You will see him there, just as he told you before he died."

The women fled from the tomb, trembling and bewildered, and they said nothing to anyone because they were too frightened.

Then they briefly reported all this to Peter and his companions. Afterward Jesus himself sent them out from east to west with the sacred and unfailing message of salvation that gives eternal life. Amen.

After Jesus rose from the dead early on Sunday morning, the first person who saw him was Mary Magdalene, the woman from whom he had cast out seven demons. She went to the disciples, who were grieving and weeping, and told them what had happened. But when she told them that Jesus was alive and she had seen him, they didn't believe her.

Afterward he appeared in a different form to two of his followers who were walking from Jerusalem into the country. They rushed back to tell the others, but no one believed them.

Still later he appeared to the eleven disciples as they were eating together. He rebuked them for their stubborn unbelief because they refused to believe those who had seen him after he had been raised from the dead.

And then he told them, "Go into all the world and preach the Good News to everyone. Anyone who believes and is baptized will be saved. But anyone who refuses to believe will be condemned. These miraculous signs will accompany those who believe: They will cast out demons in my name, and they will speak in new languages. They will be able to handle snakes with safety, and if they drink anything poisonous, it won't hurt them. They will be able to place their hands on the sick, and they will be healed."

When the Lord Jesus had finished talking with them, he was taken up into heaven and sat down in the place of honor at God's right hand. And the disciples went everywhere and preached, and the Lord worked through them, confirming what they said by many miraculous signs.

(Mark 16:1–20)

AND SO WE come to the end of Mark and the beautiful picture he paints of our Lord and Saviour Jesus Christ.

Through this book, our way of seeing Jesus has taken on a different perspective. We sought to see Him as a leader, as our leader. I pray that our hearts and minds have been shifted from seeing Jesus as just another great leader to seeing Him as a personal friend—indeed, a personal leader. He is the one we can follow.

We can have a deep and abiding relationship with Him. In coming to know Jesus as our personal Saviour and Lord, we are given wisdom, intuition, power, and an example that goes beyond knowledge to helping us achieve true life transformation. We are given access to exercising the gifts of the Holy Spirit and growing in the fruit of the Holy Spirit. We are invited to see and experience ever-increasing amounts of love, joy, peace, patience, self-control, gentleness, kindness, faithfulness, and goodness in our life and leadership.

As we read and reread this passage, we are made aware of Jesus's preparation of the disciples for this time at the end of His life and ministry on the earth. Today we would call this a time of transition and change, perhaps even a time of considering the elements of succession.

We also hear a common rebuke Jesus had given them in other situations. He admonished them for their lack of faith, or their lack of belief in what He had prepared them for. When given the good news, the disciples didn't believe Mary Magdalene.

As a leader, Jesus invited every person He appeared to after the resurrection into the great adventure of telling everyone they knew about this life-changing news. The good news was that a personal relationship was and is available to everyone who believes.

As I reflect on this journey of viewing Jesus as an amazing leader, I'm challenged to think of what it means for me. Jesus was God and also human. I am simply and straightforwardly human. He was willing to die as He led His people. I perhaps will not be asked to die for my people. More likely, I will be asked to live for my people. I have been given an example of how to live with and for my people—and this example could change the world.

You and I have been given an invitation to partake in the greatest mission that could ever be accomplished on the earth.

KALEIDOSCOPE REFLECTIONS

1. Thoughtfully record your thoughts and impressions on Jesus and how He led.

2. Which of these learnings resonates most with how you have been created and called to this great adventure of seeing the world be changed by this man's life and legacy?

3. Who do you need to invite into this great adventure, to travel together, to empower each other and to hold one another accountable for who you are, who you are becoming and what you've been called to do?

4. As you reflect on where you've come from, what you have come to understand? Describe the way you will navigate this fresh journey and describe why this is important to you.

CONCLUSION

AS A FRAGILE and sickly child, I was blessed to have Auntie Ray in my life. My mom had moved from Toronto years earlier to teach in a one-room schoolhouse in Park Siding, British Columbia. There, Auntie Ray and Uncle Law were known for housing the schoolteacher—which is such a pedantic way of describing the outrageous hospitality my mom experienced as a single woman about to embark on a new adventure.

Auntie Ray suffered with a form of arthritis which had bent her spine so that her chin was close to resting on her knees. She was physically deformed, yet her spirit and heart for others soared beyond its crippling cage. You couldn't find a more wonderful cook or seamstress. Uncle Law had created a built-in stove and kitchen sink that sat on the floor. He'd also built an area for Auntie Ray's sewing machine at floor level.

Mom lived with Auntie Ray and Uncle Law until she completed her teaching there. After Mom and Dad were married and had my sister and I, we made frequent and much-anticipated trips to visit Auntie Ray. Her hospitality created a warm space within my heart that made me feel known and treasured. It wasn't just her hugs, affection, or perseverance in the midst of her pain; it was her heart and mind, which she used to see the needs of others and seek extravagant and fulfilling ways to provide for them.

I had no idea then, but many years later I came to realize what an incredible representative she was of Jesus's servant heart. Auntie Ray lived in the way of Jesus. She had an intuition toward others' needs and she stepped in to provide for them while teaching and challenging them to be and do so much more. She taught us to pass on to others what we learned and not simply try to give back to her.

Auntie Ray sought no reward apart from making our lives better. Her spiritual life was deeply a part of who she was and what she valued most. What she chose to do came from a place of peace and rest in the Jesus she knew.

As I think back to Auntie Ray and her profound influence on my life, I go back to Mark 16. This chapter begins with the resurrection of Jesus. My Bible tells me that in most translations the chapter ends at Mark 16:8. But then I discovered the longer version, which adds twelve verses. Reading them reminds my heart of its call and purpose. I love how the post-resurrection days unfolded. They leave me with a rich and deep appreciation for the heritage of my past and the hope of my glorious future.

He is risen! Yes, He is risen indeed! This truly is the unending story of the man Jesus, who gave up heaven's splendour to come to the earth. He gave up a close, comfortable, and known life with His Father.

Throughout this book, you have become familiar with His life, worldview, emotional wellbeing, challenges, joys, and sorrows. You have perhaps embraced more deeply His great love for you and His call on your life. You have heard His mighty challenge to get out there and take His good news to everyone. You have the opportunity to give others the gift to discover for themselves a relationship with Jesus that will give them purpose and meaning—and not only that but a chance to live with Him forever.

This is the life and love we have been made for and called to:

- To serve as we have been served.
- To love as we have been loved.
- To share as has been shared with us.

- To bring hope and healing to the brokenness in our world.
- To live with eternity in mind.

Now go. Go in the power, might, and love of Jesus Christ.

RESOURCES

The Arbinger Institute, *Leadership and Self Deception* (San Francisco, CA: Berrett-Koehler Publishers, 2000).

Graham Bretherick, *Healing Life's Hurts* (Oxford, UK: Monarch Books, 2008).

Robert Clinton, *The Making of a Leader* (Colorado Springs, CO: NavPress, 1988).

Stephen Covey, *The Speed of Trust* (New York, NY: Simon & Schuster, 2006).

Leroy Eims, *Disciples in Action* (Colorado Springs, CO: NavPress, 1981).

Ruth Esau, *Self-Care Workbook*

Ruth Esau, *What-if Leadership Journal*

Daniel Golman, Richard Boyatzis, and Annie McKee, *Primal Leadership, Realizing the Power of Emotional Intelligence* (Boston, MA: Harvard Business School Press, 2002).

Jean Graves and Travis Bradbury, *EQ 2.0* (San Diego, CA: Talent Smart, 2009).

Jean Graves and Travis Bradbury, *Leadership 2.0* (San Diego, CA: Talent Smart, 2012).

Janet Hagberg, *The Critical Journey* (Salem, WI: Sheffield Publishing Company, 2005).

Janet Hagberg, *Real Power* (Salem, WI: Sheffield Publishing Company, 2005).

Bill Hybels, *Who You Are (When no One's Looking)* (Downers Grove, IL: InterVarsity Press, 1987).

D. Martyn Lloyd-Jones, *Spiritual Depression: Its Causes and Cure* (Grand Rapids, MI: Grand Rapids Book Manufacturer, 1965).

Carole Mayhall, *Words That Hurt, Words That Heal* (Colorado Springs, CO: NavPress, 1986).

Reggie McNeal, *Practicing Greatness* (San Francisco, CA: Jossey-Bass, 2006).

Reggie McNeal, *A Work of Heart* (San Francisco, CA: Jossey-Bass, 2000).

Henry Nouwen, *With Open Hands* (New York, NY: Ava Maria Press, 1972).

Greg Ogden, *Transforming Discipleship* (Downers Grove, IL: InterVarsity Press, 2003).

Richard Rohr, *Falling Upward* (San Francisco, CA: Jossey-Bass, 2011).

Lance Secretan, *Inspired!* (Hoboken, NJ: John Wiley and Sons, Inc., 2004).

Charles Stanley, *The Blessings of Brokenness* (Grand Rapids, MI: Zondervan, 1997).

Cy Wakeman, *Reality Based Leadership* (San Francisco, CA: John Wiley and Sons, Inc., 2010).

Dallas Willard, *Renovation of the Heart* (Colorado Springs, CO: NavPress, 1935).

FROM THE HEART OF THE AUTHOR

FOR OVER FORTY-FIVE years I have felt humbled and challenged to invest in those called to leadership. To create spaces for leaders to not just attain knowledge and learn, but to experience personal and professional growth that spills over into the lives of others. A space that is safe, inspiring, intentional, and open to bringing our differences together for an ever growing future focused on developing people called to lead. My work has spanned sectors such as the Church (various denominations), non-profits, and business.

The Kaleidoscope Series began with the *What-If Leadership Journal, The Intentional Pursuit of Being, Knowing, and Doing*, and continues to grow as *Shifting Perspectives: Jesus Through A Leadership Lens* is added.

Shifting Perspectives: Jesus Through A Leadership Lens, has been a joyous work that has challenged, cautioned, and inspired me as I sat with the Lord and paid attention to the way that Jesus invited, loved and lead people.

I would love to hear the ways you have used it to invest in others and what you have seen happen in the lives of others. Please feel free to check out other resources, stay in touch, follow and contact me at:

www.RuthEsau.com
Ruth@InspiredtoLead.ca

May you experience an abundance of God's grace, strength and wisdom to lead in these days.

Warm Regards,
Ruth
November 15, 2021